It's Your Problem, Not Mine

Sara Aldrich

ISBN-13: 978-1541002432
ISBN-10: 1541002431

I have tried to recreate events, locales and conversations from my memories of them. In order to maintain their anonymity in some instances I have changed the names of individuals and places, I may have changed some identifying characteristics and details such as physical properties, occupations and places of residence.

Printed in the United States of America

First Edition

To Jason and Stacie

TABLE OF CONTENTS

INTRODUCTION

Saturday, August 16, 2014, I attended a Writer's Conference at my local library. The first morning session was on memoir writing. Afterward, I went up to the presenter to say how much I had enjoyed the session. Mentioning my forty-seven year mixed marriage, I asked if she thought that would be a good topic for a memoir. She was enthusiastic about the idea, encouraging me to write my story.

Prior to that time, I had enjoyed writing as a hobby: mostly keeping a journal, writing stories for my family in a yearly *Fabric of Our Family* Christmas gift and writing letters to family and friends. I had also written an informal memoir about my career in dancing.

After that conference, I started to think seriously about writing a memoir. I joined the Wednesday night Free Writes at the library, became a member of the Rehoboth Beach Writers Guild and took three classes in memoir writing through the Guild. I made a list of twenty-five events to include in my memoir, located documents, pictures and newspaper articles, and started writing.

It has taken me two years, but *It's Your Problem, Not Mine* is the result of my efforts. Initially, the completion of my story was to coincide with our fiftieth wedding anniversary on June 13, 2017. It was to be for family only. In early 2016, I learned that a movie would be coming out in November that told the story of the mixed race couple who had taken miscegenation laws to the Supreme Court and won.

That decision came down just one day before my marriage to a black man. It seemed a sign that my story was important and should be made available to a wider audience.

Taking the summer off from my volunteer activities, I concentrated on writing. As of August 31, 2016, the rough draft was finished. Bear with me as you read the first few chapters, as I'm trying to make you see the all-white world I grew up in. After that, the story follows events through the years until 1976, when my entire family finally accepted our marriage. In between, I hope you enjoy reading about our travels in Europe and our getting settled when we returned to the States.

It has taken time to get this published. I hope you will feel as I do that it is a story that needs to be told. Many thanks to all the friends in the Rehoboth Beach Writers Guild for their support, creative input, and encouragement, and to my family for their patience. Their reading of the rough draft helped put into perspective areas that needed more clarity. Comparing memories with my husband added depth as his were often more detailed than mine. Sit back and enjoy reading our story.

CHAPTER ONE

READY OR NOT

I'm a small town Midwestern white woman married forty-nine years to a New England city bred black man. We have two mixed race children. When our son Jason was five, I dressed him as an Oreo cookie for Halloween. It was his favorite cookie, and he liked his costume. Dressed in white pants and a white shirt, he was the filling, sandwiched between two large circles cut from black poster board. Each circle had the word "Oreo" written on it along with scribbles that loosely resembled the design on an Oreo cookie. Did he recognize the significance of the costume? I doubt it. I'm not even sure why I did it. Maybe I was trying in a not-so-subtle way to say, "Look at my son. I'm proud of him." I have no recollection of any feedback from the school, neighbors or other children about the costume. Jason is smiling in the picture I took of him that day. I'm pretty sure there was no damage to his psyche because of the costume.

We also had a black and white cat named Oreo. He was an outdoor cat and a hunter. He was our daughter Stacie's cat. She had rescued him when he was a kitten, and she was seven. A family down the street had thrown him out. Stacie name him Oreo. First she kept him in a cardboard box under our carport. Eventually, he came in the house, but always preferred to be outdoors. Oreo's personality mirrored our daughter's. Both were not afraid to face a confrontation. I'd call them scrappy.

Looking back, I'm glad our daughter had spunk. It made her life easier. She was never afraid to stand up to name callers or bullies. In high school, some of her classmates didn't like her dating a black senior from a neighboring town. One student took a black jelly bean and a white jelly bean, squeezed the two together and threw them at her. Stacie told the girl, "You're ridiculous! You've known me since kindergarten. I haven't changed just because I'm dating a black man!"

When I entered into my mixed marriage in 1967, I thought I knew what to expect. In reality, I wasn't prepared at all. My childhood in that small Midwestern town gave me no contact with any people of a different color or ethnicity. The only black person I saw as a child was an elderly woman named Anna Ben Hayes who would slip into our church after the service started, sit in the back pew, and leave as soon as the benediction began.

It wasn't until years later that I learned there had once been a thriving Negro community in my home town of Oregon, Missouri. I found a newspaper clipping from the local paper *The Holt County Sentinel* that described that community in detail. "The Negro population stayed about one hundred sixty for many years. There is no history of any racial trouble of any kind. They were above average in intelligence and were very industrious. Most of them owned their own homes, and their homes were scattered here and there over town." By the time I was born the Negro community was long gone.

Many were forced to move to the cities, when the advent of the automobile took away their work with horses in local stables. The depression also cut into their jobs as household workers, laundresses and nannies. In white homes, the lady of the house took over those jobs. The businesses that supported the farmers weren't as affected. I do remember being told the Negro school was located only a block from my home. It too was gone by the time I was born.

St. Joseph, Missouri, was the closest city to Oregon. We went there every Friday so I could take dance lessons. One Friday, when I was ten years old, I remember a meeting between my father and a

Negro man. We were driving down the street in St. Joseph when my father suddenly pulled over to the curb. He rolled down the car window and called out to an elderly Negro man who was standing on the sidewalk. He was thin with grizzled white hair. He limped a little as he walked over to the car. My father got out and joined him by the edge of the road. They shook hands and talked for a good ten minutes. Sitting in the back seat, I couldn't hear what they were saying. They seemed like old friends who hadn't seen each other in years. Several times the man smiled and was animated.

Getting back in the car, my father asked my mother if she recognized the man. "That was Nat Tahl. Remember, your parents used to hire him every year to do the spring cleaning." According to the article mentioned earlier, "Nathan Tahl was the house cleaning specialist who would completely clean a house from top to bottom by himself and unsupervised." The article went on to say that Anna Ben Hayes and Nathan Tahl were "the last survivors of the colored people in Oregon." Just a word about Anna Ben. She and another girl also named Anna married the Hayes brothers. In order to know which "Anna" people were referring to, the girls took their husbands names: Anna Ben Hayes and Anna Steve Hayes.

As I write this, I remember that in third grade my class was studying clothing. There was a whole unit on cotton and the growing of cotton in the south. The class performed a skit written by our teacher called "*Cotton Pickin' Days*". It was set before the Civil War and took place on a plantation. I played the plantation owner's young daughter. Naturally, the cast included Negroes. Since there were no colored people in town and thus no colored children in the school, black face was used.

As an eight-year-old, I thought it was funny to see my friends in black face. I didn't see them as anything but the children I played with every day. They weren't colored. They were my friends. I doubt if the parents who came to see our skit thought there was anything wrong with using black face. After all, Eddie Cantor and Al Jolson had been using black face in their shows for years. In today's politically correct society, a teacher would lose her job if she attempted to use black face with the children in her class.

That is the sum total of my childhood memories of Negroes. Not once did I actually come in direct contact with any colored people. I had no concept they were different from me. I was an observer who saw no problems with any of the stories I've told here. As I grew older, I gradually began to realize that while I didn't have a problem or see the Negroes as different, many people did. As we moved into the late fifties and early sixties, the climate in the nation began to change. Eventually my experiences also changed. My high school years gave me no contact with anyone outside the comfortable white enclave that was Holt County,

Missouri. I'm sure there were Negroes in St. Joseph and other large cities, but my trips to the city did not expose me to them. I entered college at eighteen having had no experiences with anyone of a different race or ethnicity.

A little history. Missouri came into the union as a slave state back in 1820 as part of the Missouri Compromise. Maine was admitted as a free state and Missouri as a slave state. It was the first attempt at settling differences between the North and the South on the question of slavery. Many Missourians were unhappy with that decision. The southern part of the state that bordered on Arkansas and Tennessee raised cotton and had slaves. The northern two-thirds was truly Midwestern, as it had Kansas, Iowa, Illinois and Nebraska as its neighbors. The crops there were corn, wheat, cattle and hogs. No slaves, just hard working farmers. During the Civil War, that division of the state was apparent as the Union Army claimed many more soldiers than the Confederacy. My great grandfather, James Kelly, died in the Civil War as a Union soldier. He left a wife and five children on their farm near Oregon, Missouri. It was a story that was repeated thousands of times during the Civil War.

CHAPTER TWO

NEW YORK CITY

August 1958 When I was seven years old, my family went East to visit my mother's brother in New Jersey. The one memory from that trip was seeing the Rockettes at Radio City Music Hall. After taking dance lessons for a year, I was enthralled by the high-kicking dancers. I was determined to one day be a Rockette. Eleven years later, I stood at the corner of 42nd Street and Broadway. No, I wasn't in New York to try out for the Rockettes. I was there as part of a Presbyterian Church Mission Study Tour. At age eighteen and on the brink of a whole new life when I entered college at the end of the month, this tour was in the way of a send-off .

It was August, and the waves of heat from the pavement seemed to shimmer as they rose. I could feel the warmth emanating from the people who brushed against me as they rushed past. Their destinations were unknown to me, but they were moving with purpose and confidence. They were New Yorkers and used to the hectic pace of their city. The heat wasn't my only concern, even though it was making me feel hot and uncomfortable. Two girls from the tour were standing nearby, but I felt alone.

A sea of people flowed around me. People of all different colors, nationalities, backgrounds. I heard conversations in languages I didn't recognize. There was a frenetic energy that was foreign to me. The exhaust from passing taxis and the blare of their horns irritated my nose and ears. I had a sudden urge to close my eyes and clap my hands over my ears.

Ever since I saw those Rockettes, I'd dreamed of going to New York City. I wasn't here to try out for the Rockettes. I was on a very different mission. Why would the fulfillment of the dream to come to this great city not be a time of wonderment? Why was I feeling insecure and not excited? I was actually feeling a little dizzy and nauseous. Taking a deep breath, I looked toward the two girls who were with me. Like me, they were taking in their surroundings. They looked as lost as I felt. Seeing their familiar faces steadied me. We were soon joined by the rest of the tour group. Our goal that afternoon was to see as much of New York

City as we could in the free time we had. The mission we were staying at was in the Bowery, a long way from 42nd and Broadway. We were all Midwestern teenagers and none of us had ever experienced anything like this huge city. From the drunks laying in the gutters in the Bowery to the majesty of St. Patrick's Cathedral, it was all new. Even a little frightening. I didn't remember ever hearing any language in my entire life but English. The only foreigners I'd met were the Glimka's, a German family sponsored by my church when they came to the United States, and they spoke English.

Living all my life in the rural Midwest where there was very little diversity, but a great deal of emphasis on family and community, I was overwhelmed by the new experiences attacking my senses and self-confidence. In Oregon, there were concerts on the courthouse band stand. Families attended church together on Sundays. The homecoming parade drew large crowds. Backyard cookouts brought families together on a Saturday night. I doubt if most families in New York City knew what a homecoming parade was. It certainly didn't go down Fifth Avenue. Not many backyards in Manhattan for cookouts. No high school bands giving weekend concerts. Instead, there were ticker tape parades for championship sports teams. Concerts in Central Park drew thousands. It was a whole different world.

As others from the Caravan joined us, I determined I would

absorb and enjoy all these new experiences. New York was not the first stop on our tour. We started out in Gary, Indiana, moved on to Detroit, and saw Niagara Falls when we were in Buffalo, New York. All those cities were much smaller than New York City. More like the cities I knew back home. St. Joseph and even Kansas City couldn't be compared to New York City. As we headed to 34th Street and the Empire State Building, our group leader suddenly hailed a man passing by, calling him by name. As the two greeted each other with back slaps and laughter, I realized the world had just narrowed. What are the chances that two men who hadn't seen each other in years and lived thousands of miles apart would meet on a New York City street corner?

Why am I telling this story? Because that Caravan trip was a turning point in my life. For the first time, I was exposed to a world outside my white world. The poverty and crime there was not on the same level as what happened daily in big cities like New York. A drunk slept off his binge in the local jail. The poor family was helped by the local churches. A teenager went for a joy ride in a "borrowed" car. No murder, burglary, rape or grand theft auto to be found in Oregon, Missouri in the fifties.

Yes, I knew that some families sent their children to school in hand-me-down clothes and that church ladies took baskets of food to poor families, but at eighteen it didn't affect my life-style. In Gary, Indiana I had seen men out of work who couldn't feed their families. I saw alcohol make men homeless in the Bowery. When we went through West Virginia on our way home, I saw true poverty. Barefoot children. Homes with no electricity.

The people who were helped at the missions we visited weren't colored or white. They were people in need. To be fair, the colored predominated in Gary, Indiana, and Washington, D.C. Whites were more prevalent in New York's Bowery and West Virginia. What I experienced that August was my first step toward becoming a more mature and sophisticated adult. It was a small step that helped pave the way for the giant leap I made when I entered into my mixed marriage on June 13, 1967.

CHAPTER THREE

COLLEGE YEARS

1958 to 1962 As I entered college in the fall of 1958, I was back in an all white world. Northwest Missouri State College was my mother's alma mater, and my brother Robert was already a student there.

Although I was just a freshman living in the new freshman dorm, I was enrolled with a difference. Because of my dance experience, my college education was free: free tuition, free room and board, plus $250 a semester spending money. All I had to do for the next four years was teach two classes in Modern Dance each semester.

The prospect of teaching dance in the Women's Physical

Education Department didn't bother me. I had been teaching dance since I was ten years old in my studio in Oregon. What did cause me worry was the thought of going from a small town of 850 people to a campus with over 3,000 students. I was not an outgoing person at age eighteen. With mousy brown hair, freckles, and a tendency toward buck teeth, I was no beauty.

Meeting new people was always a challenge for me. What I did have was smarts. I graduated as valedictorian of my high school graduating class. I had an extensive vocabulary thanks to my English teacher mother and avid reader father. Those smarts resulted in my being rushed by Delta Zeta Sorority. A friend from high school was already a Delta Zeta. They needed members who would bring good grades. A prime candidate, I became a Delta Zeta.

One year I held an office in the sorority that involved informational and educational sessions for the membership. A lot of the topics chosen for those sessions were mandated by Delta Zeta's National Organization. One of those topics was plainly racist, although that term wasn't used in the fifties. It was my job to tell my sorority sisters that we didn't accept girls of different races. We were a white organization. Coloreds had their own sororities. No Asians, Negroes, American Indians need apply.

I did the presentation, but was uncomfortable with it. I didn't understand why we were white only. Actually the whole exercise was mute as there were no colored girls on campus. Northwest Missouri State College (NWMSC) enrolled its first colored student the year I was a freshman. He was there on a football scholarship. I saw him a few times on campus. I have no idea what his name was or if he attended more than one year. He was the only colored student I remember in all my years at NWMSC: four as a student plus two as a full time instructor.

Four years as a student flew by. My life was full of teaching dance classes and completing work on a double major (English and Physical Education). I found time to take part in the college production of *Brigadoon*, dancing the role of Maggie and helping with the choreography. I was the Queen of Misrule at the annual Christmas *Hanging of the Greens* in the women's dorm. That, too, was a dancing role. I worked with the Dance Club trying to build up membership.

Between my junior and senior years, I was encouraged to attend summer school at the University of Wisconsin in anticipation of starting graduate school there after graduation. Their modern dance department had an excellent reputation. My summer there was an important step as I expanded my understanding of the world outside NWMSC.

One of the most challenging parts of my job teaching the dance classes was evaluating students and assigning grades. Many of my students were older than I was. A few were already experienced dancers. They took my classes to fulfill their physical education requirements. Not only did I have to evaluate the students, but they had to evaluate me as a teacher. I'm proud to say that I never got anything below a B and most students gave me As. I was a good teacher.

I was aware that times were changing. The Civil Rights movement had started. Though it hadn't reached my college campus, it was only a matter of time. The 13th, 14th and 15th amendments to the Constitution passed after the Civil War gave Negroes legal status as free men. They were given citizenship and guaranteed the liberties enjoyed by all citizens. By the late 1870's, those rights were being chipped away bit by bit. No laws were passed, but the Southern states adopted policies that successfully ignored the individual rights of the Negroes.

The “separate but equal” concept was developed to keep Negroes out of white schools and other public facilities. The Supreme Court upheld that policy in 1896 with the Plessy v. Ferguson decision. It wasn't until decades later, in 1954, that the Court under Earl Warren declared in Brown v. Board of Education that public schools were to be desegregated with “all deliberate speed.” The same Court also ended racial restrictions in housing and other practices that made a mockery of civil rights for Negroes.

The Reverend Martin Luther King, Jr. assumed leadership of

the Civil Rights movement in 1956. His first success was a campaign to desegregate the public transportation system in Montgomery, Alabama. The peak of the struggle for civil rights came in the sixties. There were sit-ins, Freedom Riders, demonstrations on college campuses, voter registration drives and courtroom battles.

Safely tucked away at NWMSC, I was more aware of panty raids at the girl's dorms, food fights in the cafeteria, and creating skits for the Homecoming Variety Show than in what was going on in the South. There were no television sets in the dorms. I only read the college newspaper. Radios were used for listening to music. It was a true news blackout, especially when you were writing term papers or studying for exams. Little did I know that the man I would eventually marry was taking part in a sit-in at a Woolworth's lunch counter near his college campus in West Virginia. Selma and Montgomery were not household words on my college campus.

I graduated as one of the top four students academically in May of 1962 and received a scholarship for attending graduate school from the American Association of University Women. I had already applied to the University of Wisconsin graduate program and been accepted. I had been hired to teach dance full time at NWMSC after I graduated. It was understood that I would begin work on a master's degree in modern dance. It seemed my future was being planned for me. My previous summer at the University's Madison campus had opened up a whole new world to me. I was restless and wanting more than what NWMSC could offer me. Nevertheless, I felt I owed the college for my free education. Teaching those two modern dance classes had been easy and fun. It hadn't seemed like work. The head of the Women's Physical Education Department and other department staff assumed that I would stay on as a full time instructor. I don't remember anyone asking me what I wanted. At age twenty-two, I was just happy to have a job waiting for me when I graduated. I had received a memorandum from the College President's Office in March officially notifying me that The Board of Regents at its January meeting had approved my appointment as a teaching assistant in the Department of Physical Education for Women for the academic year, 1962-63. My salary for nine months was $4,800. Looking back I realize, they were getting a full-time instructor for less than they paid giving me free education each year.

CHAPTER FOUR

THE UNIVERSITY OF WISCONSIN

Summer School, June 1961 Strolling the winding dirt path that was the short cut to the Student Union, I stopped for a minute to gaze out at Lake Mendota. The sun glistened off the water. The lake seemed to sparkle with dots of light that danced across the waves. The path was a cool oasis from the summer sun as the tree branches created a leafy canopy overhead. I was out to explore the campus, and my first stop would be the Student Union to pick up a map.

Being outside in the fresh air was a welcome relief from the depressing atmosphere in my dorm room at Tripp Hall. Gray metal desk and bed posts, army style blankets, dull listless olive drab curtains at the one window and a small closet bulging with my clothes did not inspire positive thinking. I doubt I'd spend much time there. The room could be brightened with my personal possessions (family pictures, posters, a favorite plush cat). Just a small touch of home.

Arriving two days before my summer school classes started, I had time to settle in and locate all the important places like the dining hall, the building that housed the dance department and the Student Union. My trip from Oregon, Missouri, to Madison, Wisconsin, had been a bit of an adventure. The nearest train station was in Forest City, Missouri, (population 450) just four miles from Oregon. That station, however, was just a mail stop. Mailbags were caught on hooks. The train didn't actually stop, just slowed down. Arrangements had to be made in advance for the train to stop to pick up a passenger. Even then the stop was so brief you had to be quick or it took off without you. At twenty-one, I felt sophisticated. After all, I had traveled thousands of miles by bus on my Mission Study Tour three years earlier. I hopped right on and was on my way.

Arriving in Chicago in the early afternoon, I had to make my way to O'Hare Airport to catch a plane to Madison. My seasoned traveler persona suffered a set-back as I had no idea about bus schedules and ended up taking a taxi. I have a feeling I was "taken for a ride." Taxi drivers apparently knew a country bumpkin when they saw one. At the airport, there was no problem as I had made reservations in advance. The airplane, however, was a shock. It was a small prop plane that only held a dozen passengers, and it was my first plane ride. There were more than a few moments of queasiness and panic as we took off. I closed my eyes, gripped the arms of my seat and prayed. Once in the air, I relaxed a little. Looking down at the rolling farm country we were flying over made me think of home.

Thankfully, the flight was a short one. While Madison was the state capitol and a university town, it was not very big. I have no recollection of how I got from the airport to the University, so it must have been fairly easy. I already knew my dorm and room assignment. I just had to locate them on the vast campus. With a set of directions that had been sent and a few questions, it wasn't difficult. My self-confidence was returning.

Settling in took little time. Exploring the campus was another matter. Although there were bus routes throughout the main campus, I decided to walk. You couldn't really explore from a bus. I located Lathrop Hall on my map and headed there so I would get an idea of how long it would take me to walk from my dorm to class. Lathrop Hall housed both the Womens' Physical Education Department and the Dance Department. My first class started at 7:30 in the morning. I discovered that it would take at least 20 minutes to reach Lathrop. Days would definitely begin early. The campus was spread out over several hundred acres. Most buildings were brick or stone, many of them dating from the 1800's. The University was founded in 1848. The campus was only one mile from Capital Square and the heart of Madison, but it had grown outward through the years.

There was no comparison between Wisconsin and Northwest Missouri State College. I could get from point A to point B anywhere on campus at NWMSC in five minutes. Five minutes on campus at the University might get me to the dining hall that served several small dorms. Getting to Bascom Hill and Bascom Hall at the heart of the campus would take at least fifteen minutes. I would be doing a lot of walking that summer. With the dancing and the walking, I would be in good shape when I returned to NWMSC in the fall.

Having located Lathrop Hall, I headed toward Bascom Hall. My Aunt Edythe Kelly had told me to look for a plaque on the front of the Hall. A relative of hers named Richard T. Ely was the head of the Economics Department at the University from 1890 to 1925. The plaque was installed on the Hall in 1915 to commemorate the decision by the University's Board of Regents that exonerated Professor Ely of charges brought against him for teaching socialism and progressive thinking. The decision was a manifesto for academic freedom. The plaque read in part "it is continual and fearless sifting and winnowing by which alone the truth can be found." In some small way seeing that plaque and knowing it had a connection to my family made me feel less alone and small on this huge campus.

Back at my dorm, I decided it was going to be an interesting summer. In many ways, the campus reminded me of a miniature New York City. When I ate my first meal in the dining hall, I encountered fellow students that were a mixture of all different colors, nationalities and backgrounds. By the second day, I had met a doctoral candidate from Pakistan, an undergraduate from Mexico, and Mari, a fellow dance student from New York City.

Mari and I spent time after class that first day analyzing the prospects for a social life during the summer. She was bound and determined to catch the handsomest and most interesting man as her escort for the two months we were here. It was almost comical to see her evaluate every man who was sitting near us at dinner. That one was too tall, this one was too talkative and on it went. I was to remember later that she had no comment about a man I thought was attractive. He was a light-skinned Negro with the body of an athlete, maybe a football player. Not too tall with lots of great muscle tone. He wore a tank top that showed his physique to advantage. He was bald. It was impossible to tell if he shaved his head or was naturally bald. He definitely was a beautiful specimen of manhood. Mari didn't seem to notice.

As classes progressed that summer, it was challenging to meet new people and slowly relax as I got to know them. Hearing conversations in different languages became common. The vastness of the campus no longer intimidated me. Mari and I became good friends. We shared the dancing, but in all other aspects we were opposites. She was big city. I was small town. She was Italian. I was Irish/German. She was dark and petite. I was fair and towered four inches over her. She was definitely prettier and much more vivacious. My quieter, more laid back personality, let her shine.

I took three classes that summer. During the week there wasn't much free time. Saturday and Sunday were the days when you could enjoy all the campus had to offer. The Student Union had a popular club called the *Rathskeller*. Modeled after a German beer hall, it actually sold a special beer that was made at the University. In 1961, it was the only college campus in the country that served beer. Two years later, it would become the first campus to have male and female students living in the same dorm. One evening while sitting on the Student Union terrace enjoying a beautiful sunset over Lake Mendota, a young man stumbled onto the terrace declaring loudly to all "I am mature!" He was also drunk! I remember a young Negro girl climbed to the top of the fountain in the library square and announced, "One day I will be President!" Don't know if she had been to the Rathskeller.

All kinds of water activities were available through the Student

Union. One Saturday a friend from the dorm and I signed out a canoe and went paddling on the lake. The sunny sky turned ominously dark, and soon the quiet lake had white-caps. Neither one of us were experienced paddlers. We fought against increasingly rougher waves to get to the calmer water near the shore. It was a struggle, as we didn't really know what we were doing. Just as it started to rain, we reached the shallow water and were able to follow the shore-line back to the dock at the Union building. There had been moments when I was sure we were going to capsize. Goose bumps covered my arms as I broke out in a cold sweat. We were soon drenched and shivering. It was not an experience that made one want to venture out on the lake again. At least not any time soon!

Half way through the summer, I noticed Mari wasn't around as much. She was no longer at many of the evening meals in the dining hall. I missed seeing her every night to talk about the day's classes.

One Saturday, I left campus to go shopping in Madison and saw Mari. She was not alone. Her companion was the handsome, bald, athletic man I had admired. No wonder she had seemed to ignore him that first time. He was the one she wanted. Being from New York, she didn't care if he was a Negro. He was hers, and she'd got him!

Was I shocked when I saw them together? No. I was jealous.

She had definitely snared the biggest catch of the summer. I never learned his name. Mari was soon spending all her time outside of class with him. I saw them off campus several times, but never approached them. As far as I know, no one else realized their relationship. Mari with her Italian coloring was actually darker than he was. I've often wondered what happened to them.

In 1961, as I was watching Mari pursue an inter-racial relationship, mixed racial groups of Freedom Riders were riding interstate buses South to challenge local segregation laws. Dr. Martin Luther King, Jr. had worked successfully to have segregation banned in interstate travel. The Congress of Racial Equality (CORE) sponsored the Civil Rights activist Freedom Riders. Outbreaks of violence followed the Freedom Riders wherever they went. The segregated South was striking back!

When I returned to NWMSC at the end of August to begin my senior year, it was the same quiet campus I had left in May. Few international students, little diversity, English spoken exclusively unless you were a language major and limited choice in major studies. Having experienced Wisconsin, NWMSC was no longer my world. What was happening in the Civil Rights movement in the South was now a topic of concern for me. Would this little Midwestern college remain unaffected, or would it move on to the national scene?

CHAPTER FIVE

UNIVERSITY OF WISCONSIN 1962

Graduate School, Summer 1962 In my mind the summer of 1962 has always been "the folk dance summer." I was back at Wisconsin as a graduate student. Classes would be more difficult as I'd be taking Kinesiology along with my dance program. When I returned to NWMSC in the fall as a full time instructor, folk and square dancing, individual sports and fundamentals of dance would be added to the two classes I had been teaching for the last four years. With my Physical Education major, I had experienced all the individual sports and the square dancing. Fundamentals of dance posed no problem. It was the folk dancing that had me worried. While there had been a smattering of folk dancing in one of my classes at NWMSC, I really needed to bone up on all the different types and the countries they represented. This first summer as a graduate student, my free time would be devoted to learning as much as I could about folk dancing.

To that end, I made inquiries as to what was available on campus as far as folk dancing clubs and classes were concerned. As it turned out, folk dancing was very popular, and there would be several opportunities to join in extra-curricular folk dance activities. There were no official classes offered. I found a Folk Dance Club that met at the local Presbyterian Church right on campus. New members were welcome. They offered beginner classes and taught a new dance at every meeting. By the end of the summer, I'd be an expert folk dancer. With some folk dance experience plus being a good dancer, there was no need to take a beginners class. Doing a little research at the library would give me an idea ahead of time about what the most popular dances were from each country and whether partners were needed. There were plenty of line and circle dances that didn't require partners.

Dressed in a knee-length full skirt and a matching peasant blouse, I was ready for my first folk dance session with the Madison Folk Dancers. A block away from the church, you could hear the music coming from the hall. It was Russian and familiar. The balalaika was producing a resounding, rousing rhythm that made me want to dance. It took a minute, but I finally remembered it as the music for the Troika, a dance I had done at NWMSC. Standing in the open door of the hall watching the dancers doing the intricate steps, I remembered doing those steps two years before. The music came from a record player in one corner of the room. Throughout the evening, officers of the club would take turns announcing the next dance and putting on the music. The list of dances for the evening was always determined in advance and the records put in the proper order. It was evident that this was a well-organized group.

Chairs were lined up around the walls and tables had been pushed into corners out of the way to make room for the dancing. All windows were open and fans were placed throughout the room. Dancing is hot work, and already people were seeking out the fans to cool off. Hoping the temperatures would lower when the sun set, I stepped into the room. The Troika ended, and people rearranged themselves into small groups as they waited for the next dance to be announced. Looking around for familiar faces, none came into sight. I really hadn't expected to know anyone there, as the summer session had just started. It was unlikely I would see anyone from my previous summer at Wisconsin. Learning long ago that a smile is a great ice breaker, my face had enough beams to melt an icicle. The music started for a line dance I recognized, and I joined in. It didn't take long to feel at home with the steps. Moving freely to the music was, in itself, reason to smile.

I sat out a couple of partner dances, using the time to introduce myself to others who were gathered around the table where drinks were provided for the thirsty dancers. It was evident that the girls outnumbered the boys about two to one. For some reason, many boys considered dancing as sissy. True dancers knew being in top physical condition was absolutely necessary. I was sure the class I taught in September would have few boys. Girls would partner with girls. Boys would choose more manly classes to fulfill their physical education requirements. Luckily, there are always line and circle dances so everyone can join in. Planning to take advantage of all those dances, I looked around to check out possible partners. I'd have to wait to be asked, but those partnerless dances would let people see I knew my way around a dance floor.

Several of the boys were exceptionally good dancers. A question or two gave me the information that Fritz was the tall, blonde one with the German accent. Julius was the scholarly-looking Negro from Chicago. His glasses gave him that intellectual look, and he was thin and short. In a way, he looked like someone's younger brother. I soon learned that his looks were deceiving, as he was an expert dancer. While Fritz seemed serious as he danced and didn't smile much, Julius was obviously enjoying himself. He danced with an ease that was enviable: positive proof that you can look scholarly and be a good dancer.

More people had come in since I arrived, and the hall was soon packed. While the dance floor was quite large, there wasn't enough room for everyone to be dancing at the same time. The chairs around the wall were full of people sitting out dances or waiting to be asked during the partner dances. It was obvious that the boys realized the need to spread their services around. To give them time to rest, many of them sat out the line and circle dances. While a few of the girls danced together, most waited to be asked by one of the boys.

The next dance announced was the Hora, an Israeli line dance. The music, *Hava Nagila*, is dramatic, building in intensity. I quickly joined the line. With jumps, hops and kicks, it is a vigorous dance. Arms around each others' shoulders, the line moved around the room. The tempo gradually increased. By the end of the dance, everyone was tired, but exhilarated. So far I'd enjoyed the evening immensely. It got even better when Fritz approached and asked me for the next dance. Another Russian dance, the Korobushka, was not as complicated as the Troika. I still had to keep my mind on the steps. It was important to do well or there might not be any more partners tonight. My smile remained firmly in place so Fritz won't know how nervous I was. Pretending you're having a good time without worrying about missing a beat or stepping on your partner's toes isn't easy. The smile must have worked. At the end of the dance, Fritz thanked me and asked me to stay with him during the intermission so he could introduce me to more of the group. "Yes!"

The rest of the evening flew by. Partners were plentiful. That dance with Fritz broke the ice. I only sat out a few dances. Doing more than thirty dances in one evening was tiring, especially when most were energetic. People choose to sit out dances just to catch their breath. The last dance of the night was announced. As Julius approached me, I was very aware that I'd be dancing with the best dancer in the room. For the first time in my life, I'd be touching a Negro. He reached for my hand, and as I looked down at my pale hand in his brown one, my only thought was, "He doesn't feel any different!"

I was to dance with Julius many times that summer. He was the first Negro I really talked to and got to know on a social level. He played an important role in my understanding of the fact that not only didn't he feel any different, but he wasn't any different from me. He laughed. He worried. He studied. He walked, ate, slept and lived his life just as millions of other people of all colors and races. Just as each individual on this earth is shaped by his/her life's experiences, Julius and I shared our love of dancing, then went our own ways when the summer was over. Julius left me with the knowledge that he might be colored, but he was different from me only in how he was shaped by his life experiences.

CHAPTER SIX

"FREE"

September 1965 Free! That thought kept winging its way through my mind as I packed the big trunk that sat at the foot of my bed. Free to move forward without any strings attached. Free to find out what I was really capable of. Free to leave academia behind after nineteen years. Free to have fun and explore the world. I was off to Germany to work as a civilian employee of the United States Army. Graduating from Northwest Missouri State College (NWMSC) in 1962 and beginning work as a full-time instructor in the Women's Physical Education Department, I lost many of the freedoms I had enjoyed as a student. There were strict rules at the college about staff fraternizing with students. Even though I still had many friends among the students on campus, including my sorority sisters, I couldn't socialize with them. Contact with students was strictly limited to the classroom and occasional counseling sessions. My social life became nonexistent. I looked to the other faculty for possible social opportunities. The average age of most of the faculty was probably around fifty, and they were all married. Not just the age difference, but my single status made it almost impossible for any social relationships to develop. There was one bachelor in his forties, but he was as dull as the subject he taught (higher mathematics).

Attending my first faculty meeting, it was evident that no free thinking or disagreeing with the administration was allowed. My department head had instructed me on how I was to vote on any issues that were presented for approval. That didn't sit well with me. I could think for myself and didn't need anyone to tell me how to vote.

I had my teaching job at NWMSC and was grateful for the free education I had received as an undergrad. My two summers at the University of Wisconsin had shown me what academia was like on a large liberal campus. It was very different from NWMSC. My decision had been made to give the college at least two years of full time teaching as payment for the free education they had given me. I could see myself in the same dead end job ten years down the road if I didn't follow up on that decision.

It didn't take me long to realize that those years would be boring and frustrating. I certainly didn't want to be an old maid like Dr. R. who taught anatomy and kinesiology. Or maybe like Mim, who taught swimming. She was what in the sixties was called butch. My rebellion started slowly. I quietly began to meet some of my student friends in off-campus coffee shops. I began dating an Air Force veteran who was back in school on the G.I. Bill. We usually left campus and spent weekends in either his hometown or mine. There were times when he came to my apartment in the evening. Jim was several years older than me, and I had met him when he took one of my ballroom dance classes. When that class ended, he asked me out, and I accepted. We saw a movie together. That first date led to a real relationship. He had a striking head of auburn hair with a matching goatee. He was fun and the first serious boyfriend I had ever had.

As an act of rebellion, I included Jim in the work on a Dance Club production that was to be presented as part of the college's Festival of the Arts in April 1964. That *Evening of Dance* was the first dance concert presented at the college in more than five years. To this day, I consider that production the highlight of my dance career. I received letters of congratulations from the President of the College and the head of the Women's Physical Education Department. I gave Jim a special thank you for his work on the concert in the official program. I always felt seeing us working together on the concert was what alerted the staff in my department that we were dating.

We were discovered. I was firmly warned by the Department Head that continuing to date a student could result in my dismissal. It didn't matter that he was older than me or wasn't in any of my classes. He was a student. We continued to date after that warning but were more careful not to be seen by anyone. I had originally planned to spend the next few summers working on my master's degree at Wisconsin. After the warning about dating Jim, I decided to speed up the process and requested a year's leave of absence to finish my degree. As I left for graduate school in June 1964, I knew I would never return to NWMSC. I wasn't exactly sure how, but I vowed never to go back. To his credit, Jim wrote me letters almost every day that summer. Knowing I wouldn't be returning in the fall, I sent him the one and only "Dear John" letter I've ever written. He was more serious about our relationship than I was. It still was hard to break up.

During my year at Wisconsin, my major changed from modern dance to physical education. That major also included health and recreation. Dance was no longer an important factor in my future. It had served me well for almost twenty years, but I was ready to move on. My emphasis now was on recreation. My plan was to pursue a career in that field when I finished my masters. To that end I contacted my first cousin, Barbara, in California who had spent two years working in recreation for the Special Services Division of the Army in Germany and got information on how to apply.

I submitted my resignation to NWMSC in April. Upon graduation in August, I was heading to Europe as an NGS 6. GS was the designation for civil service employees. What the N stood for is not in my memory bank. Usually, Special Service hires started as NGS 5s, but because of my masters, I got the 6 ranking. That meant more salary, and the job of Program Director at whatever Service Club I was eventually assigned to. I would be planning recreational activities for enlisted men in the army. My new career in recreation was off to a good start.

So here I was Free. I'd had all my shots, obtained a passport and made travel arrangements to Washington, D.C. All that was left was packing. Deciding what to take with me and what to ship in the trunk wasn't all that difficult. As I had no idea where I would be stationed in Germany, the packed trunk would stay behind until I contacted my father with my new address. The two suitcases I was taking with me contained everything I needed to survive until my trunk arrived. I know I packed all my winter clothes in the trunk and hoped cold weather wouldn't arrive until my trunk did. It could take several weeks for it to catch up with me.

Yes, I was Free. It was a wonderful feeling. I had fulfilled my obligation to NWMSC. Now I could follow my own dreams.

Europe awaited.

My personal freedom, ironically, followed years of the pursuit of freedom in the Civil Rights movement. The 1964 Civil Rights Act outlawed discrimination based on race, color, religion, sex or national origin. The 1965 Voting Rights Act signed by Lyndon Johnson prohibited literacy tests or any form of economic coercion in voter registration. 1963 saw Dr. Martin Luther King, Jr.'s *I Have a Dream* speech. The moving words at the end of the speech come from a Negro spiritual: "Free at last, Free at last, Great God a-mighty, We are free at last."

How could I ever feel that my little struggle to break free compared in any way to the great struggle going on all across the country? Only now, in 2016, do I truly appreciate that the Civil Rights movement created the climate in the United States that made my mixed marriage possible.

CHAPTER SEVEN

THE PENTAGON

September 1965 The big departure date was September 13, 1965. Thirteen had always been a lucky number for me. Fifteen years later, our thirteenth wedding anniversary actually fell on a Friday the thirteenth. In 1965, I felt it was lucky to be flying to Washington on the thirteenth. Even better was the fact that I would be staying at the Willard Hotel. My father's name was Willard. Everything seemed to be pointing toward a good beginning to my new adventure.

I checked in a day early so I would have time to do a little sight-seeing before the Army claimed me. It was crisp and cool for September in D.C. My sweater felt good as I climbed the steps to the Capitol Building. Entering the rotunda and looking up at the high ceiling, I felt small and insignificant. The fresco by Brumidi is one-hundred-eighty feet about the floor and is breathtakingly beautiful. My eyes wandered to the people around me. Suddenly, my gaze was caught by an attractive man standing a few feet away. He was a red head with a trim beard. He reminded me of Jim. He had a sophisticated manner that was intriguing. We nodded and smiled. It was as if a magnet drew us together. I'm not sure who spoke first, but before long we were chatting as if we were old friends. Other than the red hair, he turned out to be nothing like Jim. He was more serious, taller, and knew a lot about history.

We ended up spending the day together.

We took in the huge paintings in the eight niches around the rotunda. We wandered through Statuary Hall where I located the statues for Missouri. We went on to the Lincoln Memorial and the Washington Monument and parted ways at the end of the day. I never saw him again, and I don't remember his name. It was the perfect prelude to what was to come.

Early the next morning, the Army collected its newest employees from the Willard. We were transported by bus to the Pentagon, where we spent a very busy day of orientation and getting fitted for our new uniforms. Like the military, we received two blue winter uniforms and two lighter blue summer uniforms, plus navy heels and purse, white gloves and a hat that was worn cocked so the tip was in the middle of the forehead. We were warned to make sure there was room in our suitcases for our uniforms. It was a tight squeeze, but I managed to get them in. The winter uniform was a two piece suit worn with a supplied white blouse. The summer uniform was also two piece with the top having short sleeves, no blouse needed. The uniforms were not free. Payment would be taken out of our first few paychecks.

If you've never been in the Pentagon, it's an unbelievable experience. Built during World War II, it was completed in 1943. It has five sides, five floors above ground, five rings or corridors around the inside, five entrances with each office door having four numbers and one letter on it, for a total of five. Thus, the name: Pentagon. More than twenty thousand people worked there. The outside ring was the only one with windows and housed the senior officers. Despite having seventeen miles of corridors, we were told people who worked there could get to any location in less than seven minutes.

The place was a rabbit warren, and without our constant military guide, I would have been one very lost rabbit. I felt dizzier than when I was standing on that street corner in New York City in 1958. There was a crispness and no-nonsense atmosphere that made you think there was only one speed to get through the day. That speed was fast! By the end of our two days of orientation, I at least knew where the entrance we were using was located. We actually stayed pretty much in one area, but were given a brief tour in the beginning.

The military had been fully integrated for twenty years, but I don't remember seeing many Negroes in the Pentagon. Of course, I wasn't looking for them. There were so many people in the halls and public areas that they all blurred together. It was all very formal and precise. No camaraderie evident.

September 16, I was on my way to Heidelberg, Germany on a chartered TWA plane that landed in Frankfort. For the first time in my life, I was outside the United States. A feeling of isolation grew as we boarded the bus that took us to the Headquarters of the United States Army in Europe (USAREUR) in Heidelberg. There, we would get our actual assignments and military orders. We had traveled in uniform. It felt strange to wear a hat and gloves. The two-inch high heels were uncomfortable. Would I ever get used to wearing heels? While we were civilian employees of the army, we were essentially governed by military rules and regulations. We greeted officers as Sir, but at least we didn't have to salute. It was evident that I had entered a whole new world that would take some getting used to. I refused to be homesick. At twenty-five and with a graduate degree, it wasn't like my first day at Girl Scout Camp back when I was ten.

Sara Aldrich, September, 1965

CHAPTER EIGHT

LETTER FROM HEIDELBERG

September 17, 1965

Dear Dad,

They certainly haven't given us much opportunity to mingle with the natives, but then we're all so glassy-eyed and bone tired, the only thing we're interested in is a good night's sleep. We left Washington, DC at 1:30 Thursday afternoon and drove by bus to McGuire Air Force Base in New Jersey. It was a four-and-a-half hour drive, and we had one rest stop. When we arrived at the air terminal, our boarding passes, immunization records and passports were all checked, which meant standing in line for about thirty minutes. Then we stood in another line for thirty minutes to get our luggage checked and weighed. After all our panic, I don't think there was a soul who was overweight. I can tell you some of us had been pretty worried. The third line we stood in was at the cafeteria, and that was the longest wait of all. The lines in the military are worse than those in college – if possible. Our flight was a chartered TWA Boeing 707, and it was pure luxury compared to what it would have been on a military transport. There were stewardesses, meals served, pillows, etc. The whole works.

We took off at exactly 9:00 p.m. EDT Thursday and were in the air almost eight-and-a-half hours. That's a little longer than usual because there was fog in Frankfurt, and we circled waiting for it to clear. We got off the plane, walked two steps and boarded a military bus which took us to the spot where we picked up our luggage and went through customs. It was approximately 10:00 a.m. Frankfurt time when we arrived. There is a five hour time difference. Then we boarded another bus for Heidelberg. By this time, we were almost walking in our sleep. We struggled manfully to keep awake so we could see a bit of the German countryside, but most of us lost the battle and fell asleep. It took just a little over an hour to get to Heidelberg, where, after a very brief introductory meeting, we were told we were free until 8:00 Monday morning.

I'm sharing a room with a girl named Mary Ann, who is in Library Science (we had singles in Washington), and the minute we got to our room we went to bed. We slept from 2:00 to 4:30

that afternoon, then got up long enough to go to the officers' club for dinner. We're now back in the room, and even though it's only 8:30 p.m., we're getting ready for bed. Will write more tomorrow when I'm wider awake and have seen something of Germany beside U.S. Army installations.

September 18, 1965

I sent you a postcard from downtown Heidelberg today, but you can't say much on a post card. We got a good night's sleep and had breakfast at the officers' club again. Then we ventured forth with $10, a lot of expectations and not a few qualms. Heidelberg nestles at the foot of beautiful, forest-covered mountains. (The ride from Frankfurt was through very flat country, and I had begun to be disappointed until we saw the mountains around Heidelberg). It is divided by the River Neckar, which is completely navigable with the help of twenty locks. The old city of Roman and Medieval times was centered around the Holy Ghost Church (which is now Protestant). On the mountain-side above the city, the Prince Electors built their huge castle. The castle was destroyed by wars and fire in the seventeenth century, and the walls and part of the interiors have been restored. This castle and the legendary University of Heidelberg are the city's main attractions, but it is also one of four German cities that remained untouched by the bombing during World War II, so it has retained much of the old world charm that so many cities lost in rebuilding after the war.

Heidelberg has narrow winding streets, beautiful flowers, cobblestone walks, lovely little shops and restaurants, trolley cars and a quaintness that can only be found in Europe.

That first venturing forth took more courage than you might realize. We know nothing of the language, and we didn't have any idea where we were going except to downtown Heidelberg via the trolley. Lady luck smiled on us, however, when the conductor on the trolley spoke English, changed our money for us and saw that we got off at the right spot. He really made our day for us. Now we felt ready to brave all of Germany. The first plunge is always the hardest.

Our first purchase was postcards. Then we found the post office and wrote and mailed them on the spot. Next we found out about bus tours of Heidelberg, walked through one of the big department stores, bought some candy and had lunch at a German restaurant. By this time, we were old hands at counting German money and making ourselves understood. I keep saying "we", and I mean Mary Ann, myself and another girl named Helen. After lunch, we walked down more narrow back streets, strolled through Bismarck Park and down by the River Neckar. Then we returned to the main square to take the bus tour of Heidelberg. It lasted two hours and took us through the university and the castle. By this time, we were pretty tired, so we took the trolley back and went to bed until 8:00 p.m., when we were once again on our way back into Heidelberg for a night on the town. We stopped at the *Red Ox Inn* which is quite famous. But they weren't serving food, and we wanted dinner. We were down in the university area and all the places were filled with German students drinking beer, singing at the tops of their voices and having a whale of a good time. We wandered around and soaked up atmosphere until 12:30 in the morning and then took a taxi back to the base. Our whole day cost us less than $5, and that includes meals, tour fare, trolleys, taxis, tips, etc.! We were really amazed!

Tomorrow, we plan a boat ride down the River Neckar and a cable car ride up to the top of one of the mountains, where we'll have dinner at a restaurant. It should be another full day. It's 2:00 a.m. So I'd better get to bed. But first a word about the German people. They are not openly friendly as most Americans are. They are courteous and always polite when you ask them something. But for the most part they simply answer your question and that's it. No friendly, "Where are you from?" or "How do you like Germany?" Of course, there are exceptions, like our trolley man and one or two others.

I like Heidelberg, I like Germany, and I like the Army. Guess I'm in pretty good shape. Share this letter if you want to, and give my best to everyone. We get our permanent addresses on Tuesday. Take care. Love, Sara Beth"

That letter was the first of more than one hundred seventy-five letters and postcards I sent to my father during the two-and-one-third years I was in Germany. He saved every one of them. You will find quotes from those letters throughout the rest of this book. What a help they have been to my own memory. I also have been a letter saver. You will find excerpts from letters he wrote to me, plus letters I received from both family and friends.

When I arrived in Frankfurt, it was the first time I had been outside the United States. It was a strange feeling to realize I couldn't just pick up the phone and call home. International calls were very expensive. I only made one call to the States in all the time I was overseas. That was to my father on his birthday July 14, 1966. That nine-minute call cost $36.00. In case of emergency, all calls would go through the Red Cross. My father and I each bought small tape recorders and sent tape recorded messages back and forth once a month. It was good to hear his voice, and much cheaper than a phone call. I don't remember feeling homesick, but I was very aware that I couldn't just go home for a weekend.

CHAPTER NINE

THE ASSIGNMENT – 98TH GENERAL HOSPITAL

September 1965 A letter written to my father on September 20 said "the fun has stopped and the work has begun. We had orientation sessions from 8:00 in the morning to 5:00 p.m. Were they ever dull!"

Finally, on the second day we were given our assignments. I was going to 98th General Hospital, a small military hospital located in Neubrucke, Germany. It was in the western part of West Germany close to the French border. I was to be the new Program Director at the Service Club, which meant I would plan a full calendar of daily activities for the enlisted men who worked in the hospital. Everything from pool tournaments to cooking classes to

USO entertainments would be on the calendar.

Most Service Clubs had three or more staff, but Neubrucke was so small there were only two: the Club Director and the Program Director. That meant one girl was alone in the club every other night.

I would have two weeks to learn the ropes from the girl I was replacing. Presently, there was almost no organized programming going on as the outgoing Program Director was quiet and shy. She was not one to get up in front of guys and run a program. Service Clubs opened at 1:00 and closed at 10:00 p.m.. That's a long day to fill with activities. My job would be to revamp the monthly calendar, filling it with a variety of programs that would attract young, enlisted men, many of them between eighteen and twenty years of age. Quite a challenge.

I was to learn that the enlisted men assigned to the hospital for the most part had above average intelligence. Many had some college education. They worked in operating rooms, the emergency room, with medical records or in admissions. They were medics who were given responsibilities that affected people's health and well-being. A higher level of programming that would challenge them was what they wanted to find at the Service Club. The guys who worked in the kitchen or janitorial services would be content with playing pool or ping pong, listening to music or playing cards and board games. The rest would expect and demand more. This was why I was being brought in. I wasn't being paid to check out equipment! Having learned where I would be going and what was expected of me, I was eager to get started.

The next day, I was to take the train to Mainz, where I would be met by my supervisor and driven to Neubrucke. At 6:45 a.m., I was waiting at the bahnhoff (train station) for the train. I was in full uniform, including the white gloves. Having been warned that German trains always run on time and stops are short, I was ready to board quickly and had my two suitcases gripped tightly. My regulation bag securely on my shoulder and my umbrella hooked over my arm, I was poised to board as soon as the train stopped. The door opened, I lifted my foot, and my two-inch navy high heel fell off into the black void between the train and the platform. I froze! Staring down I could see the shoe wedged tauntingly against the track. My only thought was, "If I miss the train, what do I do?"

Suddenly from behind me, a hand grabbed the umbrella off my arm, thrust it down to the track, hooked the shoe, pushed me and my suitcases onto the train, and threw the shoe and umbrella in after me. The door closed, and the train started to move as I desperately sought my balance and tried to see my rescuer. To this day, I have no idea where my guardian angel came from, but as I found a seat, I thought what had just happened was a good omen for the start of my new life. Someone was definitely looking out for me.

CHAPTER TEN

THE MEETING

September 23, 1965 As we traveled by car from Mainz to Neubrucke, I saw more of the German countryside. The mountains were low and tree-covered. Many little villages nestled in the valleys between mountains. The red roof-tops were bright in the sun as we passed by. In my September 24th letter to my father, I described what I saw. "There are small narrow valleys with streams and rivers running through them, and each valley has one, and usually more, little villages. This is the real Germany! Here is where you see the narrow cobblestone streets, the old, old houses, the farmers plowing with horse (and cow) drawn equipment, etc. .....There's a wealth of lovely scenes for the photographer. Just hope I don't get carried away."

Neubrucke, itself, was a tiny village. I doubt if it appeared on most maps. It was a stop on the main railroad, so it wasn't completely isolated. 98th General Hospital was so big you would have been able to put several Neubrucke villages within its perimeters. Twelve miles away was Baumholder, a United States Army Base that trained NATO forces and housed a variety of military units, including tank units. The base was one of the largest in Germany, and the hospital was basically there to serve Baumholder.

My first full day in Neubrucke was crisp, cool and clear. I wrote my father that "I've never felt better in my life. There's something in this air that really stimulates me."

Dressed in full winter uniform, I reported for work at the Neubrucke Service Club on September 23, 1965. Ann S, the girl I was replacing, took me on a tour of the facility and introduced me to all the staff. Besides the office, there was a pool room, two music rooms, a combination lounge and card room, and a photo lab. In addition to the service club girls, there were three paid employees: a secretary, a housekeeper and an artist. Over fifty years, later I don't remember names. I do remember the secretary was the American wife of an MP (military policeman) stationed at the base. The housekeeper was the German wife of one of the medics. The artist was also German and spoke excellent English.

He designed the monthly activity calendar and made large posters advertising planned trips and upcoming major events.

I wrote my father that "The hardest part now is learning all the technical aspects, official procedures and complicated paper work. Every time you need a paper clip, you have to fill out a purchase order and submit it a month in advance! Never have I seen so many technicalities. Everything has a different officer's signature and a special place where it has to be turned in. I suppose six months from now, it will all be old hat."

It wasn't just the official procedures that taxed my brain. It was the small differences between the United States and Europe. The metric system as opposed to the decimal system used back home caused some confused moments. When you bought a bag of apples, it was weighed in grams not pounds. You purchased liters of gasoline, not gallons. The distance between towns was figured in kilometers, not miles. The German monetary system took some getting used to. The Deutsch mark was their main currency. In 1965, a mark was similar in value to an American quarter. Thus four marks roughly equaled one dollar back home. I spent many minutes trying to figure out exactly how much something cost in American dollars when I was shopping on the German economy. Then there was the pfennig, which was similar to our penny. Fortunately, U.S. dollars were used on the military base. The Army also had what I considered silly procedures with dates and time.

All military reports had to be dated 7 July, 1965, not July 7, 1965. Official times for the afternoon and evening hours were not 1:00 p.m., but 1300 hours. Thus, 2000 hours was 8:00 p.m. Figure that one out.

As we neared time for our dinner break, we were introduced to two sergeants who came in to the Service Club when they got off duty and worked as volunteers. The first was Joseph G. As far as I could tell, he made sure the guys didn't get rowdy in the pool room. He took over checking out all the equipment and helped us close the club at night. I was to rely on him many times during the next few weeks. The second was Sergeant Pat Aldrich, who ran the photo lab as a volunteer. He had learned his considerable photography skills at the Service Club in Ft. Leavenworth, Kansas, when he was stationed there.

First impressions are not always true or lasting, but in this case they proved to be exactly right. High cheek bones, chocolate skin (somewhere between milk and dark), dreamy brown eyes, a tailored dress uniform, and a confident walk that said, “Look at me.” He was the complete package: easy on the eyes. He was introduced as Pat Aldrich, and it wasn't until months later that I found out Pat was a nickname because he was born on St. Patrick's Day. After he left the room, I told Ann, “I'm going to have to watch myself with that man. I'm very attracted to him.”

Pat, Circa 1965

CHAPTER ELEVEN

SETTLING IN

October/November 1965 Learning a new job. Meeting dozens of new people. Exploring the new world surrounding me. That was what I faced during my first two months at Neubrucke Service Club. I like to think I handled it all with panache. One of the dictionary definitions of that word is “spirited self-confidence.” My letters home certainly reflected that I was full of confidence. Sixteen letters to my father during those months gave a blow-by-blow account of events that ranged from a major theft of cash at the Service Club to an invigorating day of hiking the mountains around Neubrucke. The theft happened on my day off. It was payday, and our housekeeper had cashed her husband's check. The cash was in her purse in the kitchen when the theft happened. I was told the Club was filled with MPs who interviewed everyone and had them sign statements. As far as I know, the thief was never caught.

I wrote in detail about the people that were most important to me. Strangely enough, Pat Aldrich, while mentioned frequently, did not stand out as being extra special. My first mention of him came in an October letter, where he was listed with several others as being among my favorites. More often than not, Pat was mentioned with his friend Steve. The two seemed inseparable. A longer description appeared as follows in a later letter that month. "Pat runs the photo lab, which is located in the same building as the Service Club. He is a Sergeant and is in charge of the Admissions and Discharge section of the hospital. He has four years of college with a major in psychology. I enjoy talking to him a lot, and he has been a big help in and around the Club at various times. He runs the photo lab on a purely voluntary basis during his off duty time. He's 29." Nothing there to indicate he was any different than the others mentioned in the same letter. All very factual. In fact, my descriptions of several were more full of personal insights.

Writing about Joseph G. (who I mentioned in the last chapter), I called him the recreation assistant at the Service Club. "He's 32, married, has four kids and is just about the greatest guy around, with the exception of my own Dad, who's the greatest, bar none. Joe has taken me under his wing.

"He's really like a big brother, and he's sure taking care of me. He also takes excellent care of the Club. I don't think it could run without him. Joe is very highly trained in his field: heart surgery. He is the only man in USAREUR (United States Army in Europe) who can run the machine for open heart surgery. When he's not working heart surgery, he's in charge of the electrocardiogram."

Also in the same letter, I wrote this about Sergeant P., who had earlier given me a single yellow rose. "Sergeant P. is the ladies man of the group. He's the only one who's handsome, suave and extremely attractive. The exterior creates the impression of a shallow playboy, but underneath is a true southern gentleman who is sensitive and understanding. He has excellent taste and is the best dressed man I've seen in many a year. He's in charge of the Outpatient Clinic at the hospital and during the big Inspector General inspection we had a couple of weeks ago, his section was highly praised and he got a letter of commendation from the post commander." Wow! I'm sure when reading that, my father thought I was going to be dating Sergeant P. in the very near future.

Although I did have a very brief fling with him, the fact was I was more impressed by Sergeant Aldrich than Sergeant P., but I was being cautious on all fronts and didn't want to tip my hand too soon that I was pursuing him. To that end, I enjoyed outings with one of the officers I met at the Officers' Club. I went dancing with Captain S. in October and to an Oktoberfest with him the following week. I described him as a friend who could be a valuable escort on a friends basis only.

My first weekend off (I got one a month), I went by train to Idar Oberstein with Norm, one of the enlisted men. Norm was an accomplished musician and played several instruments. He and his friend John spent their time in the music room playing instruments and listening to music. He was a premed student before being drafted. He was serious and perfectly safe. No romantic thoughts there. Idar Oberstein was the gem cutting capital of Europe, and there were fabulous jewelry stores and a museum that was quite interesting. It was also known for a church built into a rock high on one of the hills, *The Church in the Rock.* So far, I'd managed to enjoy myself with several escorts while quietly spending more and more time with Pat Aldrich at the Service Club.

My trunk arrived the second week in October. At last I had some winter clothes. Days had been quite cool. But after the sun, went down it was downright cold. Closing the Club at 10:00 meant I was walking home in temperatures at least twenty degrees lower than when I opened at 1:00. It took me two days to completely unpack. I discovered quite a few needed items that weren't in the trunk so a request for a care package went out to my father. There were some things I couldn't find at the Post Exchange (PX) or on the German economy: things like navy shoe polish (my shoes were getting pretty scruffy being worn almost every day), my favorite lipstick and even Mentholatum. Back home, he was busy with the fall harvest. When his brother went pheasant hunting in South Dakota, my father described himself as the "Chief Herdsman of the Shorthorns." Because he loved fishing, I told him that the fishing in the rivers and streams around Neubrucke was great because they were well stocked with a variety of fish. While I loved to fish, I never did get to try my hand in all the time I was in Germany.

In another letter, I tried to answer my father's questions about my everyday life including where I was living and where I ate my meals: mostly at the hospital snack bar when working or at the Officer's Club for lunch. On days off, I often ate in German restaurants and had become fairly proficient in reading the menus. I shouldn't have been too cocky as one time I thought I was ordering roast beef and got tongue! My living arrangements were on the fourth floor in the nurses' quarters where I had two rooms and a bathroom. Climbing all those stairs at 10:30 at night when I was tired, was a challenge. I informed him that if any of my letters looked like they had been opened, they probably had. The CIA did spot checks of the mail going to and from military bases outside the United States. I assured him that if I enclosed anything, I would mention it in the letter.

A letter in early November described the first snow fall. "We had our first snow this morning. Actually, it was more sleet than snow, but it made me think winter had arrived. Tonight is the coldest it's been so far. We'll have a hard frost, and the last of the leaves will be gone. It was still beautiful and autumn-looking today with the mountains clinging to the few colorful patches of leaves that the winds were doing their best to snatch away. Once the leaves are gone, I want snow to get here fast."

Answering a request from my father on how to pronounce Neubrucke I wrote: "The first three letters *neu* are pronounced *noye* like Noyes Blvd in St. Joe but without the s. Bruck is pronounced like the word brook. The final e is pronounced like a long e as in key. So you have 'noye brook e'" The English translation is New Bridge.

While work took up most of my day, I managed to enjoy social events late in the evenings. Not arriving till after 10:30 and still being in uniform, I must have really stood out. At the get-acquainted party at the Officers' Club on October 22nd , I was conspicuous among all the cocktail dresses. At the Halloween Party, I was the only one not in costume. I only stayed an hour. I fit in better at the lively floor show at the NCO Club earlier in the month. I went with a batch of the guys from the Service Club. Pat and Steve were in the group. We shared a table, and they walked me home at 1:00 a.m.. I managed to make it to church the next morning but had trouble staying awake during the sermon.

My life revolved around all the G.I.s that came to the Service Club. Attendance at the Club went from packed at the end of the month to sparse at the beginning after pay-day. "Business at the Club is really slow right now. It's the first of the month and all the soldiers are rich from pay-day. We have maybe ten to fifteen guys in the club at night. Everybody else is out drinking, gambling or wenching and probably all three. Most of them will have hangovers in the morning and not a few of them will be broke. Once they've spent their money, they come back wanting to be entertained. We really do a roaring business just before pay-day when they're broke. A soldier and his money are soon parted." We often had three hundred and fifty in the club at the end of the month.

Probably the event that was the most fun and cost no money came in November. It was the hiking in the mountains I mentioned earlier. "Yesterday was my day off, and I had a day that was almost perfect. . . . At 12:30 I met Don R., and we went hiking: three hours up and down mountains, through brush, across streams and over rocks. As usual, it had rained during the night, but we had boots on. What we couldn't traverse wasn't worth the effort anyway. We did some pretty fancy sliding going down a couple of those mountains. That mud can sure be slippery. When climbing, once or twice I took one step forward and slid back three.

It was so warm we didn't even wear coats. Don was in his shirt sleeves, but I had on a sweatshirt. It was the kind of day that you just had to be outside. We almost ran into a deer, we found some blackberries and stopped to eat a few. We stumbled onto a lonely solitary grave with a beautiful crucifix guarding it and the remnants of what had been lovely floral offerings. It was an old grave, but the flowers had been brought recently. It was almost as if this were a shrine where the local people come on pilgrimages. I walked on soft pine needles and swung from tree branches. I saw an old German war bunker, and found a spent shotgun shell. I waded creeks and looked out at the world from the top of the mountain. It was a beautiful day, and we returned from our hike tired but refreshed."

One of the hardest things was saying goodbye to the men who were transferred or shipped home. The first soldier I lost was Barney. He had already been at Neubrucke for thirty-three months, so he knew he was going home soon. He was kind of a special friend. "He was the first fellow I met at the Service Club when I arrived. He made it his business to take me on a tour of the post and made me really feel at home." It was easy to get attached to the fellows when you worked with them every day. By the middle of October, I had already said goodbye to several guys, but Barney was the first I'd been close to.

I discovered it was hard to write about my experiences in Germany. Reading one of my letters, I'm sure people couldn't get a true understanding of all the things I saw and did. More especially, they wouldn't know how I felt about them. I continued to write every week, hoping that those back home would in some small way understand what a truly wonderful experience I was having.

CHAPTER TWELVE

THE PURSUIT

Fall 1965 Maybe this chapter should be called "The Chase" because that's what I did from the time I admitted how attracted I was to Pat Aldrich. My strategy was to slowly infiltrate myself into his time at the Service Club. To that end, I began stopping by the Photo Lab whenever he was there. I had learned how to develop and print black and white film when I was working on my thesis at Wisconsin. That allowed me to ask intelligent questions about the lab, to seek help in refreshing my skills and to request advice on buying a camera. I asked him to teach me how to use the enlarger so I could do 5" x7" and 8" x 10" black and white pictures. He was a good teacher.

The Photo Lab was quite large with a studio, work room and dark-room. The whole developing process of chemicals fascinated me. Pat always put his chemicals in a sink of water just warm enough to heat them to the level he wanted. The developer, the stop, the fix and the wash, when used properly, gave you your negatives. I soaked up all the details and advice that Pat offered. The dark-room held the four enlargers. I never felt comfortable in that room. The red light made it look and feel eerie. Wanting to learn how to enlarge pictures so I could be with Pat, I spent more time than I wanted in there. But it wasn't romantic at all as far as I was concerned.

On my days off, I often spent time in the photo lab. I had a new camera recommended by Pat, and I wanted his help in learning how to use it. If the lab wasn't busy, I would find Pat and Steve listening to music. Folk music was becoming very popular, and Pat's favorite singer was Joan Baez. He also liked Judy Collins and Bob Dylan. I asked my father to look for a certain Baez record that Pat didn't have. The very next letter I said “forget it” as I found it locally. That was my first gift to Pat. The record player they were using belonged to the Service Club, but the records were all Pat's. He had quite a collection.

He liked to play pool, so I made sure to spend time in the Pool Room when he was there. At the first of the month, when things were slow, I got him to teach me to play pool. I didn't really care about playing pool, but it got me considerable one-on-one time with him. I also challenged him to a ping pong game, which I won. Since I taught table tennis at NWMSC, I should have given him a handicap. After the Service Club closed, Pat and Steve often went to the NCO Club (Noncommissioned Officers' Club). If there was something special going on at the NCO Club, like Mexican Night, a floor show or some of the guys jamming, I was usually able to get myself included when they headed there.

The Club didn't serve fancy food. There was Mexican food once a week because the cook was Mexican. The french fries were popular. Most people didn't want a full meal that time of night anyway. Remember, I never arrived before 10:30. The NCO Club offered very different types of activities than the Service Club. There were slot machines, a bowling game, a jukebox and plenty of beer. The lights were always turned down low and the music loud. As long as I was sitting with Pat and Steve or other guys I knew from the Service Club, there was never a problem. Fights didn't break out often. In fact, not once was there an altercation when I was there.

It was at the NCO Club that I first danced with Pat. While he was a great athlete, he was a terrible dancer. Contrary to popular belief, not all black people can dance. Pat was one who had two left feet. He kind of shuffled around in one spot. Having taught ballroom dancing, it was a disappointment that he would never be even a good dancer. I vowed that I wouldn't try to teach him to dance. He would probably run away screaming. There were too many other good qualities about him. I could overlook the poor dancing part.

I worked hard at chasing Pat, considering him mine from the start. I engaged him in conversation at every opportunity to find out as much as I could about him. I learned he was from Connecticut, had attended college in West Virginia, had been stationed at Ft. Leavenworth, Kansas before 98th General Hospital. He smoked (yuck), but not in the Service Club. He was a leg man. That was definitely a plus. With all my dancing, I had a very nice pair of legs. He liked pot roast and meat loaf, my type of cooking. He was an excellent athlete, having played sports all his life. He had played on the Neubrucke softball team that summer and on both the football and softball teams at Leavenworth.

It turned out we shared tastes and preferences in many things. We both liked classical music. Bowling was a favorite pastime. Popcorn was addictive. Utrillo and Rodin ranked high on our list of great artists/sculptors. Then, of course, there was our shared interest in photography. We were also opposite in some areas. No one can be completely compatible. Being from New England, he loved lobster and all seafood. I was allergic to shellfish. He liked gin and tonic and beer. I didn't drink. He was a Gran Prix automobile racing fan. I couldn't even drive a stick shift and didn't see the fascination for funny-looking cars going a hundred fifty miles an hour.

Pat was an avid reader. Some his favorite authors were Ayn Rand, Ian Fleming and Robert Ludlum. His taste in movies ranged from *Citizen Kane* to French and Russian films with subtitles. He enjoyed opera and had a collection of opera records that he listened to frequently. In short, he was a man of excellent taste and high intelligence.

Sometimes, it was difficult to see Pat alone because he was popular and was usually with a group of friends. Steve in particular was like an extension of Pat. They worked together in the photo lab, hung out together at the NCO Club and traveled together when they had weekend passes. While Pat was the one I was interested in, I made a point of joining the two just as if there were no ulterior motives on my part.

Everything about Pat fascinated me. His beautiful brown eyes mesmerized me. Sometimes, I was so caught up in them I had to look away. It was too much. His expressive hands were exquisitely shaped, and he used them effectively when he talked. His intelligence was evident in his ability to converse on any topic extensively. History, politics, movies and sports were just some of the areas where he displayed a vast amount of knowledge. The Trivial Pursuit game hadn't been invented yet, but he would have aced all the questions.

Before long, Pat and Steve seemed to expect me to join them at the NCO Club. It was at the NCO Club that we first heard Beatles records. They were popular in Europe long before they invaded the States. Steve, being an intelligent person, caught on to the fact that my interest was in Pat. He didn't just step aside so I could be alone with Pat more often, but he did occasionally join friends at other tables. Once Pat and I became a couple, I wondered if Steve resented the loss of his exclusive friendship with Pat. He never gave any indication that he did.

My long weekend for November was coming up, and I had thought to go to Vienna. When I heard Pat and Steve planning a trip to Paris that same weekend, my mind quickly changed. Not very subtly, I began to talk about how I would like to see Paris. My hints paid off, as without my having to ask, they invited me to go with them. It seemed that my pursuit was going to pay off. I had great expectations for that trip to Paris.

The more I knew about Pat, the more I was certain that he was special and would be important in my life. It wasn't that I was thinking long-term. A relationship between us would certainly have obstacles. I had officer status. He was an enlisted man. He was colored. I was white. Having gone through a situation before where I dated someone (Jim) that was off-limits, I had a feeling a relationship with Pat would not be easy. That didn't deter me. Pat was a gentleman. His mannerisms and qualities of personality fascinated me. In short, I liked everything I knew about him. Paris would be the perfect testing ground for what might develop in the weeks to come.

Pat and his camera, circa 1966

CHAPTER THIRTEEN

PARIS – FIRST DAY

November 1965 It was my second weekend pass since starting my job at the Service Club in September. In October, I had stayed local and explored Idar Oberstein. But! Who could turn down an invitation to go to Paris with two of the most interesting G.I.s at 98th General Hospital, especially since I had finagled the invitation in the first place.

While Pat was the object of my attention, Steve deserved more of a mention. He looked like a blonde California surfer. He was from California, but I didn't know about the surfing part. What I did know was that he was twenty-two and worked as an operating room technician. He was a very talented artist and had great potential in many ways. He had two years of college majoring in art. There was never a dull moment when Pat and Steve were around. I anticipated a fascinating time with them in Paris. The City of Lights awaited.

Do Not Go To Paris In November! At best, it's empty of tourists but also empty of the vibrant life I expected in Paris. No little sidewalk cafes, no beautiful flowers on every street and no lovers holding hands and strolling slowly down broad avenues. It was brown everywhere, no color at all. It was damp and cold, and people rushed along, hurrying to get inside where it was warm. But in November 1965, it didn't matter if it was cold and damp. I was twenty-five and going to Paris with Pat and Steve.

Windblown snowflakes struck our faces Saturday morning as we made our way to the train station (bahnhof) to catch the train to Paris. Wearing boots, heavy coats and gloves we were dressed for the second snow of the season and the first serious one. There was already more than an inch on the ground when we boarded the train. We were optimistic the weather would improve. Our positive attitude paid off. By the time we got to Paris at 2:30 p.m., it was just cold and overcast. No snow on the ground. The guys had been to Paris in July and knew their way around. We headed to the Latin Quarter on the Left Bank. Our destination was a little hotel where they had stayed the first trip. The name of the hotel is not in my memory bank, but I remember it was tucked in between other buildings on a narrow winding street. The facade was certainly not imposing. The neighborhood was typical of the student area where it was located. Cafes and bistros, bookstores, small markets and shops abounded.

I rented a single on the ground floor. Pat and Steve were together on the fourth floor. We dumped our luggage and went out to see as much of Paris as we could before night descended. I had just succeeded in learning my way around German money. Now I was challenged with the French franc. It was worth about twenty cents to the marks' twenty-five cents. Converting from dollars to francs in my head taxed my brain, especially when I was dealing with old francs and new francs. I don't think I ever really understood the difference.

Our first stop was the Eiffel Tower. We wanted to get to the top and see Paris laid out before us while there was still enough daylight to take pictures. Late on a cold Saturday afternoon, we didn't have to wait long for the elevator that took us to the top. Not being one to enjoy heights, I looked out rather than down. The rooftops of Paris, the imposing government buildings and museums, and the bedded down for the winter gardens stretched out before us. I wished I could see it again when the sight would have been full of color and activity. Yes, there were cars, buses and even bicycles on the streets below, but few people. Cold and windy at the top, we didn't stay long. The guys had seen it all before. I think they went just to please me. They pointed out the Louvre, Invalides, Le Arc de Triomphe and Notre Dame all visible in the distance.

Having heard from people back at the Service Club who had been to Paris that Parisians can be condescending and even rude, it wasn't long before I experienced it for myself on the street below the tower. There was a sidewalk vendor selling postcards and souvenirs, and I picked out some postcards of Paris. The vendor completely ignored me and my efforts to get his attention. My "pardon"s and "excusez moi"s may have been said with a heavy accent, but with three semesters of French in college, I knew they were the correct words. When he finally deigned to acknowledge me, he was both condescending and rude. The people back in Neubrucke were right. He did take my money, but seemed reluctant to do so. Just the first of several similar experiences during the short time we were in Paris.

Our next destination was the Arc de Triomphe which was only a few stops away on the Metro. Having very little experience with subways, my first ride on the Metro wasn't that pleasant. The car seemed to bump and sway as it sped along. And it was noisy! I was definitely more comfortable with trains, buses, cars and even the trolleys in Heidelberg. I remembered feeling much the same discomfort on the few subway rides we had taken in New York City in 1958. By the time we left Paris on Monday, though, the

Metro was my friend. It had taken us all over the city, depositing us in the right spot every time. Of course, having Pat and Steve there as guides made it easier. Pat, especially, seemed to be looking out for me. Steve was busy eyeing everything from an artist's point of view.

Napoleon ordered La Arc de Triomphe built in 1806 to honor his Grand Armee. In 1965, it was the largest Arc in the world. He didn't live to see it finished, but his body passed under the Arc when he was taken to his final resting place at Les Invalides. When Pat was in Paris in July, he and his friends went up to the observation deck for a fantastic view of Paris. In November, I wasn't ready to climb 284 steps to the top of the Arc. I was content to study the sculptural groups that represented military victories, the sculpted roses on the ceiling and the busy traffic that swirled around the Arc from the twelve Avenues that fed into the Champs Elysee. The French Tomb of the Unknown Soldier lay under the Arc. It was lit by an eternal flame. The Kennedys had visited in 1961. Jackie was impressed by the eternal flame and, in 1963, ordered one for Jack's grave in Arlington.

Leaving the Arc, we walked a short distance down the Champs Elysee. In my eyes, it was much more lavish than Fifth Avenue in New York City. The center divider would have been lush and green in the summer. The shops were upscale and expensive. So far, Paris was living up to my expectations.

The cold drove us back to the Metro, which took us to Le Place de la Concorde. The largest square in Paris, it has the Champs Elysee on one end and the Tuileries Gardens on the other. In the center is the Obelisk of Luxor decorated with hieroglyphics. More commonly called Cleopatra's Needle it was a gift from Egypt. Two fountains flanked the obelisk. It was at Le Place de la Concorde that the guillotine was set up during the French Revolution. King Louie XVI and Marie Antoinette and hundreds of others were executed there. As we walked around the square, I kept thinking of Charles Dickens' *Tale of Two Cities: "It was the best of times. It was the worst of times."*

The sun had set, and it was getting dark. After another quick look around the area, we once again boarded the Metro to return to the Left Bank. There would be more time to explore the next day.

Exhaustion was quickly catching up with us. It had been a long day. We picked a little bistro for dinner, as we needed sustenance. While I have no memory of what we ate, I know my first meal in Paris was an experience I wouldn't soon forget. After all, I was in Paris. How could it not be special? Sitting around a small table, we soaked up the atmosphere. All around us were people talking softly in French. Most were couples, some holding hands. They were young, probably students at the Sorbonne. Pat had his camera but refrained from taking pictures. The Parisians would not have appreciated that intrusion by a tourist. I'm sure there was crusty

French bread with the meal. It has been a favorite of mine since that first time in France. We discussed our plans for the evening and the next day. So many things to see and so little time. We didn't want to waste a minute of our time.

Deciding to go clubbing, we located a jazz club in the Latin Quarter that was featuring an American blues singer. Parisians have always loved American jazz and blues. Many artists from the States have gotten their start in Paris. Think Josephine Baker in the thirties. Tonight we would be hearing Memphis Slim. We were looking forward to an entertaining and relaxing evening. Pat especially was a jazz lover. The Modern Jazz Quartet, Miles Davis and many other jazz artists were found in his record collection.

In the Latin Quarter, many of the clubs were located underground. Walking down narrow, dark stairs, you could hear the music floating up faintly from below. Once in the club, you had to go down more stairs to get to the level of the stage. It wasn't a large area, but it was packed with wooden tables, chairs that proved to be very uncomfortable and what seemed like hundreds of people. The tiny tables were just big enough to hold drinks and ashtrays. We quickly grabbed a table when a couple got up to leave. Steve pulled over a third chair from a nearby table, and we sat back to enjoy. Most everyone seemed to be chain smoking. Pat got out his Benson and Hedges and lit up. The table next to us had two ashtrays overflowing with butts. No one was talking. All were concentrating on the blues music coming from the stage. It was my first time hearing live music in a club. Blues wasn't my favorite kind of music, but what I was hearing was enthralling and moving. Plus it wasn't all blues. Different kinds of music and rhythms came from that stage. I found my toes tapping at times.

I had never been in a situation where the air was actually swirling with blue smoke. It moved slowly around our table, and seemed to be in rhythm with our breathing. Before long, my eyes began to burn. Then tears started streaming down my face. The guys were engrossed in the music and didn't notice my distress. I knew I had to get out into the fresh air. I said Pat's name softly, but he didn't hear me. When I reached out to tap his arm, I accidentally knocked my drink over right into his lap. That got the attention of both Pat and Steve. We hurried back to the hotel. Although Pat's trousers were brand new, he was gracious in accepting my apologies.

I was fully recovered from my smoke reaction by the time I got to my room. It was the first time we had returned to the hotel since checking in that afternoon. I hadn't really looked at the room when I left my suitcase. When I opened the door, I got a shock. It was like a black hole. The weak light from the hall showed a chain hanging from the ceiling light in the room. Pulling the chain revealed a single bare light bulb hanging from the ceiling. The room was no bigger than a closet with not a single window in sight. But most important, there was no heat! I was shivering. Of course, the tiny bathroom was clear down at the end of the hall. The narrow single bed was as hard as a rock. The stairs were right outside my door, and I could hear people going up and down them. To my ears, they seemed to be stomping, and it was after midnight.

Pat and Steve had gone straight up to their room, and for the first time I realized just how alone I was. My breathing became shallow, and I found myself gulping for air. I was shaking, and the room was getting darker and smaller, closing in on me. I snatched open the door and raced up the stairs to their room. I intended to spend the night sitting up in a chair in their room. Steve opened the door and stared at the mad woman standing before him. My breath coming in short spurts, I tried to get out the words to tell them how frightened I was. After a perfectly wonderful day full of new and fascinating experiences, where had this panic attack come from? True, I had never envisioned myself all alone in a cold, damp room in Paris' Latin Quarter, but I had also never seen such a shabby, tiny hotel room with no amenities. Welcome to Paris. I imagined the stomping feet on the stairs as intruders. What exactly did I know about this part of Paris? In my mind, it seemed filled with shady characters who were capable of all kinds of evil doings.

Sitting me down, Pat and Steve finally got me calmed. Pat convinced me that I was in no real danger and would be perfectly safe in my room. They were firm that I couldn't spend the night with them. Even though no one would know, they still worried about my reputation. Pat escorted me back to my room and waited while I used the bathroom. He handed me the large, old-fashioned key and instructed me to lock myself in, put the single chair under the door handle and not leave the room until he came to get me in the morning. Did that make me feel better? In a way it made me feel safer. Pat said good night, and I turned the key in the lock. Thus ended my first day in Paris.

CHAPTER FOURTEEN

PARIS – DAYS TWO AND THREE

November 1965 Paris was still damp and cold. I had survived the night and was dressed in layers of the warmest clothes I had. A long-sleeved blouse, a pullover sweater, plus a cardigan were layered under my wool winter coat. I was waiting for Pat and Steve. Then I remembered we would be visiting museums that day. Surely they would have some heat! Museums tend to be cool. What to do? Dress for indoors or outdoors? Indoors won. I took off the cardigan, and was just putting my coat back on when Pat and Steve arrived. True to his word, Pat had knocked on my door earlier and called out a cheery “Good morning,” just checking to make sure I was all right. I hadn't been sure how to greet them after my meltdown of the night before. This morning, I was embarrassed that I had given in to imaginary fears. I decided to use Pat's cheerful greeting as my guide and acted as if the events of the previous evening hadn't happened.

A small neighborhood bistro provided our morning repast. As we opened the door, we were greeted by warmth and the tantalizing aromas of brewing coffee and freshly baked bread. I was beyond hungry. A delicious omelet, two light and fluffy croissants and a cup of steaming hot chocolate later, I was ready to tackle the day. Disappointment awaited as we were out and about much too early. None of the museums in Paris open early in the off season. There was also a problem with some museums closing on certain days of the week or being shut for renovations.

What to do for two hours before any of the museums opened? I was beginning to wish I had dressed for outdoors. We lingered in the bistro as long as possible, but when we started to get frowning stares from patrons waiting for seats, we ventured out into the cold. The Louvre had been everyone's first choice of museums, so we headed in that direction. The Metro stop let us out by the Jardin des Tuileries. At the entrance, we stopped to look across the Place de la Concorde to where we could see the Eiffel Tower. It looked stark and lonely as it loomed over the city on a cold dark day.

Maybe it was because we were cold. Maybe it was because we were disappointed that our morning plans were delayed. Or maybe it was just because we were young and in Paris, but suddenly we began to laugh. Steve and I started running and being just plain silly. It was like we were playing a game of *Statues*, as we struck poses. Holding them, then changing to move to another area and another pose. His Nikon always at the ready, Pat took several pictures. Being the oldest of the group, he must have thought he was dealing with two adolescents. The gardens were almost empty of people. Who knows how observers might have reacted to our antics? As we settled down, I realized all that running around had warmed me up.

Sara and Steve, Paris, 1965

I wrote my father that we spent most of the daylight hours in museums. In the Louvre, "I saw the Mona Lisa, Venus de Milo, and the Winged Victory." I described it as the most famous art museum in the world. It was also the largest and the most visited in 1965. It would have taken days to see it all, and we only had a few hours. Originally the palace of the French kings, it became a museum in 1793. My only other experience with a famous art museum was in Chicago in 1962 when I was given a personal tour by a curator of the Chicago Museum of Art. He was the brother of my dance instructor. The Louvre was much larger, and without a guide, I felt I was in danger of wandering around aimlessly. It helped that Pat and Steve knew their way around from their previous visit. They were able to get us to the most popular works of art without getting that lost. It also helped that the museum wasn't crowded that early on a November morning. We saw some of the extensive Egyptian collection but spent most of our time with the Greek and Roman sculpture and the paintings of the masters.

Not sure how many miles we had walked, but we were ready to sit down and have lunch at a cafe near the Louvre. I remember a simple meal of onion soup, bread, cheese and a coke. The guys had wine. You didn't drink water in Europe unless it was bottled. The coke even tasted different than it did in the States: not as sweet. I never did learn to drink wine, as it went straight to my head. Beer and I had never gotten along either. Too bitter. Pat liked German beer even though it was served at room temperature, but he didn't care for French beer.

We headed for Les Invalides Museum after lunch but didn't stay long. It housed Napoleon's tomb and military exhibits. I found it dark and depressing not like the open airiness of parts of the Louvre. Pat and Steve probably found it more interesting than I did. I wasn't a soldier. The third stop on our museum tour was the Rodin Museum. There were two Rodin Museums in Paris, but we went to the one that was Rodin's home, Villa des Brillants in Meudon. The other museum was located at his workshop in the city. French sculptor Auguste Rodin was the creator of the famous *The Thinker* and *The Kiss*. *The Thinker* was located in the extensive garden along with many of his other sculptures. *The Kiss* was inside the museum itself. It was also inside that I discovered a small statue called *The Eternal Idol*. I showed it to Pat. We both fell in love with it. If it had been for sale, we would have ransomed our souls to buy it. I settled for a black and white photograph which I intended to have framed.

Rodin was an art collector. His home housed a collection of paintings by artists such as Van Gogh and Renoir. The museum wasn't that large when compared to the Louvre. It was extensive enough that we would have liked to stay longer, but the afternoon was rapidly waning. We still had the Museum of Modern Art to see. How we ever thought we could do justice to any of these four museums in one day was beyond me. By the time we arrived at the last one, I was exhausted. Not having slept that well, I was ready for a nap. No such luck.

Steve, the artist, was in his element. He practically dragged us from room to room, commenting intelligently on the paintings, sculptures and other works of art we were seeing. Not having any real interest in modern art, I soon begged off and sat down to rest. Pat stuck it out far longer than I did, but he too soon admitted fatigue. We sat and let Steve continue his explorations. Discussing what we had seen that day, we agreed that the Rodin Museum was our favorite. His sculptures were so realistic, his topics timeless, his talent true genius.

Our stomachs told us it was time for dinner. We made our way to a family-run Italian restaurant that Pat and Steve knew from their first trip to Paris. I felt truly blessed to have them as my guides for my initial visit. They sure knew their way around. The restaurant was located on the Rue de Nations close to our hotel. It was a little bit of Italy in the heart of the Latin Quarter. I remember colorful murals of Italy on the walls and tables covered with red and white checked tablecloths. The Italian family greeted Pat and Steve with cries of recognition and even some back slapping and hugs. Pat might have been the only colored person that had been in their restaurant since he was there in July. The Negro population in Paris in 1965 was minuscule. Most restaurants, shops and tourist attractions probably didn't see many unless they were U.S.

military.

The restaurant wasn't crowded, as most Parisians ate late. We got lots of personal attention. One of the sons spoke some English, and we managed what passed for conversation with the family. While they spoke French and Italian, we, like most Americans, only spoke English. My college French was almost worthless. I did manage to convey to them that the food was delicious. We spent two hours over our meal, enjoying every minute of it. Staying far away from any jazz clubs, we went to a British movie. At least it had English subtitles.

Again memory fails me, but since I did write to my father that we saw a British movie, it must be true. I might exaggerate a little in my letters, but I don't make things up! As our second day in Paris drew to a close, I found I wasn't dreading our return to the hotel. Somewhere along the way, I had realized that while Paris was new, exciting, and very big, it was a city like most cities: crowded and busy, with its share of good and bad. If it weren't for the lack of heat, the hard bed and the cold water bathroom, I might actually get a good night's sleep.

We had to catch an early afternoon train back to Germany, but we spent the next morning exploring Montmartre with its narrow side streets and art shops. While in November the artists were not outside painting, we admired their work in the shops. I bought some Utrillo prints. I would frame them along with my Rodin picture and have a little corner of Paris in my two rooms back at 98th General Hospital.

Like many before us, we gazed in awe at the beautiful white stone church Sacre-Coeur, which sat at the highest point overlooking Paris. The white walls seemed to gleam in the bright sunlight. The gloom of the previous two days was gone. Paris, stretched out before us, was sparkling and no longer brown. It was a perfect way to say goodbye to the city. We didn't have time to climb the hundreds of steps up to Sacre-Coeur (Sacred Heart) but vowed to return to Paris and do just that. And we did in 2015.

We managed a quick bite to eat before rushing to the Gare to catch our train. It had been a whirlwind trip, and I left Paris with the feeling that I hadn't even scratched the surface. Settling into our seats on the train, Steve promptly fell asleep. Pat and I sat side by side on the seat across from him and spent the entire ride back talking. One of the summers I was at the University of Wisconsin, he was at Camp McCoy near La Cross, Wisconsin. He was stationed at Ft. Leavenworth, Kansas while I was teaching at Northwest Missouri State College just sixty miles away. Strange that Pat and I had to go half way around the world to meet.

Pat had looked after me our whole time in Paris. He made sure I was comfortable and enjoying myself. His attentiveness was endearing. By the time we arrived back at the Neubrucke bahnhof, I knew I wasn't just attracted to him. I was falling in love with him.

CHAPTER FIFTEEN

COLOGNE, GERMANY

December 1965 Change! Things had changed since our Paris trip. Subtle differences that most people wouldn't notice. Warm, smiling eyes. A gentle touch on my arm or shoulder. Standing closer so we were almost touching. Then there was the kiss. A soft gentle touching of lips when we were alone in the dark room. Never again would I think of a dark room as eerie. Pat was seeing me as a woman, not just a friend.

I made sure my body language and responses let him know his advances were welcome. Touching him was never a problem. Leaning in to get closer was a natural reaction whenever we were in close proximity. With him standing closer and me leaning in, it was a wonder we didn't collide. Smiling to myself, I decided the chase was all but over. Only one more important obstacle to overcome.

Exploring the pleasures of sex without actual intercourse! That had been an important part of my relationship with Jim, the Air Force veteran I dated back in 1964. No penetration. That was the best birth control. So technically, at age twenty-five I was still a virgin. I wasn't just falling in love with Pat. I was in love with him. It wasn't difficult at all for me to decide that he was the one!

Our next long weekend pass came the first week of December. For the first time, Pat and I would be traveling alone. No Steve to chaperon. Our destination was Cologne, a cosmopolitan city on the Rhine River. While the city suffered severe damage during World War II, the famous Gothic cathedral remained intact. By mutual consent we only booked one hotel room. Being a novice in clandestine affairs, I was nervous and not a little afraid. Before long I realized that we weren't just stealing away for a weekend of sex. We were in Cologne to see the sights and enjoy our time together. The sex would come, but at the proper time.

I wrote to my father that "Cologne was absolutely wonderful. We couldn't explore too far on foot in this cold, rainy weather we've been having, but we managed to see quite a bit. We went through the cathedral the very first thing. We also saw the new modern opera house. We were disappointed that we couldn't get tickets, because they were performing Tchaikovsky's *Nutcracker*.

"Saturday, we walked all over the main shopping area. It was jam-packed with people doing their Christmas shopping, and all the Christmas things were out in the stores. The streets were beautifully decorated. Sunday morning we went to a very nice art museum and lost ourselves there until our train left at 2:30. As usual there really wasn't enough time to see even half of the things there are to see."

Of course, there was no mention of the loss of my virginity on Saturday night. That experience was one I would never relate to anyone. Only Pat, who shared it with me, knew how important it was and how beautiful. We loved each other that night. No other words are necessary.

CHAPTER SIXTEEN

BELGIUM

January 1966 We were a couple. In the beginning, we had to hide how we felt about each other. No holding hands or hugs. I couldn't treat Pat any different than any of the other guys in the Service Club. What a relief it was once everyone knew we were a couple.

That month, our weekend pass took us to Antwerp, Belgium. The chief seaport of the country, it was also the diamond cutting capitol of Europe. We knew that Peter Paul Rubens was buried in the cathedral, and many of his most famous works were to be found there. We looked forward to exploring the city. The weather, however, did not cooperate. We got off the train to find a blizzard in progress. We barely made our way to a hotel right across the street from the bahnhof or Centraal Station, as it was called in Belgium.

About all we saw of the city was the Centraal Station, which was actually a most impressive building, even seen through the snow from the hotel lobby. The down comforter in the hotel room was great to snuggle under, and snuggle we did. Body heat also kept us warm. Skin against skin. In the beginning, it was enough to just be close and feel. Knowing there's more, increases the anticipation. No need to rush. We weren't going anywhere in the blizzard that was roaring outside.

Other than the snuggling, the most memorable thing about our trip to Antwerp was the dining room in the hotel. It was in that dining room that we had the best meal of our entire time in Europe. Fifty years later, I described it to our children in my annual "Fabric of Our Family" book. "The meal was served by a distinguished elderly waiter who wore white gloves. We felt like royalty. The service was that impeccable. We feasted on Chateaubriand with Bearnaise sauce. It melted in our mouths. We've had Chateaubriand many times since, but none can compare with that meal in Antwerp." We never made it back to Antwerp. Peter Paul Rubens and his art had to bow to nature's might.

April 1967 We did get to Brussels, Belgium, the next year. That was one weekend when we didn't travel alone. Ingrid, a teacher at the hospital elementary school, and Bob, who was a Specialist 4th Class at the hospital, invited us to join them on a trip to Brussels. Bob was a tall, handsome Negro.

Ingrid was a blonde, blued eyed American of Swedish descent. They were still at the friendship stage and didn't want to travel without chaperones. That meant that Ingrid and I would share a room. Ditto for Bob and Pat. Pat and I hadn't had separate bedrooms in months.

We couldn't leave Friday until after I got off work at 10:00 p.m. Bob had a car. As we drove through the night, we passed a sign that indicated the sight for the Battle of Bastogne in World War II. Being a history buff, Pat was disappointed we wouldn't be able to visit the sight. It was quite a lengthy trip to Brussels. By the time we got there, it was the middle of the night. The city was closed down and quiet. All the hotels we passed were dark until we got to the town center. There we found a brilliantly lit hotel with a doorman ready to help us with our luggage. He was in uniform, and like our waiter in Antwerp, wore white gloves. He even spoke English. That should have warned us right there, but we were so tired that we just wanted rooms.

Taking a good look at our rooms the next morning, we realized that we were not going to like the bill when we checked out. The carpet was plush and deep. The bathroom counters were marble. The room service brochure didn't have prices listed. All signs of a four star establishment. Four star hotels were definitely not in our budget. Going down to the lobby, we saw glass cases filled with diamond necklaces and Rolex watches. We practically sank up to our ankles in the carpet. When we saw our bill, we went into shock. No credit cards in 1966. We quietly withdrew into a corner of the lobby and pooled our resources. After paying the bill, we were left with very little money for the rest of our visit.

Getting the car, we drove around trying to find a small hotel we could afford. Knowing it would be bare bones, I still insisted on heat and hot water. No more of my Paris nightmare. We finally found a hotel at the end of a narrow street full of shops and little bistros. We checked in early and went off to see Brussels. We spent a great deal of time in the Grande Place, an open square that was surrounded on three sides by Medieval guild halls that were exquisitely carved and richly gilded. The fourth side was the city hall topped by a statue of St. Michael.

There were vendors selling fruit, flowers and vegetables. All were dressed in peasant costumes, the ladies with full gathered skirts and puffed sleeved blouses. The men wore bell-bottom style pants and long, full-sleeved shirts. We could imagine the merchants, carpenters, bakers, etc. that would have come out of the palatial guild halls in Medieval times. We spent a few of our guilders on cheese, fruit and bread for our lunch/dinner. Not far from the square, we located the famous Manneken Fountain, a twenty-four inch bronze statue of a boy urinating. The people of Brussels called him their oldest citizen, as the fountain was erected in 1619. He was affectionately known as the Manneken pis. Can't say I was that impressed, but if you went to Brussels, it was a must see. It was that famous.

Brussels is known for its fine lace. I had brought money with me to buy lace to use for the sleeves of my wedding dress. I refused to let that money be used for anything else. I got the lace. We survived without that money.

Like all European cities, Brussels had its cathedral, which we visited. It wasn't as famous or impressive as the one in Cologne. The four of us walked around until we found a park where we could sit and eat what we had bought from the vendors. We made sure to save some for latter.

As it got dark, we retreated back to our hotel. The busy little street full of shops and bistros was completely changed. The ground floor shops were all closed. The second floor windows were open and brightly lit to reveal "women of the evening" displaying their wares. Our hotel was in the "red light" district. Our rooms were usually rented by the hour. Turned out prostitution was legal in Brussels!

CHAPTER SEVENTEEN

TRAVELS

All through 1966 It was the travel year. Whether they were day trips or longer weekend excursions, we managed to see much of Germany together. You get to know someone quickly when you travel with them. I don't remember a single falling out during all our trips together. Occasionally, we would strike out on our own or with other friends. I wrote to my father, that I "spent all day in Worms soaking up history about Martin Luther." In March, my friend Ann S. and I drove to Spain in Ann's VW Beetle. We traveled through France both going and coming. Burgos, Madrid and Barcelona were major stops, but Toledo was my favorite. Attending a bullfight in Barcelona gave us a true feeling of Spain, as did seeing Flamenco dancers.

Pat and Steve were in Copenhagen in May. Pat said that the home of Hans Christian Anderson was like a fairy tale itself. Unfortunately, Steve got sick on the trip, so they didn't see as much as they would have liked. They stayed in youth hostels. On the way home, they made a stop in Amsterdam. That was their last trip together.

As Pat and I traveled together, we got to know more about each other. Each trip, we revealed a little more of ourselves. I'm not sure who said "I love you" first. It was probably me. While Pat can converse on multiple topics at length, he wasn't one to talk about his own feelings. More often than not his actions revealed how he felt. A slow, lingering kiss, a hug or even putting his arm around me as we walked told me he loved me.

Day trips close to Neubrucke for Pat and I included a boat ride on the Rhine River and a visit to Nuremberg. The little towns along the Moselle River provided opportunities for us to soak up the German culture. Our favorites were Bernkastel and Cochem. The Moselle Valley was known for its white wines. Vineyards cascaded down the steep hillsides, ending right at the edge of the river. Half-timbered houses abounded in Bernkastel. A medieval market square and the fabled pointed house were photographed by us just as they had been by thousands of tourists from all over the world.

Cochem, in the heart of the Moselle Valley, had a neo-Gothic castle perched on the hill above the town. Reichsburg Cochem (Cochem Castle) featured a Witches Tower used for witch trials. The guilty were tossed out the window. The view from the castle was breathtaking. The winding river, the lush green vineyards and the red roofs of the town of Cochem were laid out below like a mosaic.

Another favorite city was Trier. Germany's oldest city, it was founded by the Romans in 16 BC. The ruins of the Constantine Baths, the 20,000-seat amphitheater and the majestic Porta Nigra drew us back to Trier many times. The most famous relic in Trier was the Holy Tunic, said to be the robe Jesus was wearing when he died. It was only exhibited every few decades. We were never there at the right time.

In January, I informed my father that I would be buying a Volkswagen in April. "I've finally decided it's almost imperative to have a car over here. The car itself will cost $1,100 to $1,200, and the insurance will be about $200 a year." I arranged to pick up my new green VW Beetle on April 1st . It was a stick shift, and I had no idea how to drive one. Pat gave me a few lessons, but I was not comfortable with the clutch and shifting gears. I purposely picked the April 1st date to get the car thinking winter would be over. It snowed on April 1st, and I drove all the way home in 2nd gear. I soon became proficient with the stick shift but never forgot how tense I was driving home in the snow with my new car.

Pat beat me to the punch, though, as in March he bought a snazzy little English sports car, a black Triumph Spitfire convertible. With his leather driving gloves, dark glasses, and the top down, he drove the Autobahn like it was Le Mans. We brought both our cars back to the States when we returned home in 1968. Having cars greatly facilitated our many day trips around Neubrucke. No longer did we have to rely on train schedules. With our new transportation, we went to Holland to see the tulips in March and to Switzerland to see the Alps in July. In September we returned to Paris for five days, choosing to drive my VW Beetle.

As we traveled through Germany and neighboring countries, I discovered that Pat was actually more romantic than I was. He was the one who wrote little messages expressing his feelings. He inspired me to respond in kind. Our love was shared not just on a physical level, but also through notes and even poems.

We could be in a crowded room with distance between us. Pat would seek me out with his eyes. It was if I could feel him looking at me, pulling me to return his gaze. He was a strong, silent person who quietly drew me into his sphere. Though I was the one who pursued him in the beginning, he was the one who had the calm resolve that kept our relationship growing.

In June, we were on our way in Pat's Spitfire to see a 1,000 kilometer automobile race at the Nurburgring, Germany's most famous race course.. A white car passing a truck on a curve ran us off the road. As Pat swerved to avoid the collision, a tire blew. The car flipped over and landed crosswise in a ditch. We were hanging by our seat belts with our heads in the ditch. Neither the car nor the truck stopped, but others who witnessed the accident stopped. They actually lifted the car, turned it over and were amazed to find us unhurt. They had expected to find us crushed.

The accident happened near Hahn Air Force Base. Several of our rescuers were stationed at the base. After we dealt with the German police, we were driven to Hahn by military police. We were well taken care of and spent the night before taking the train back to Neubrucke the next day. It was truly a miracle that we weren't injured. Pat had a small scratch. Our guardian angel was watching over us that day. Pat's poor Triumph went back to the dealer he had bought it from for repairs. It had a bent axle, as well as other damage.

We didn't allow the accident to stop our excursions. We visited Heidelberg again, spent a weekend in Baden Baden, explored the ruins of Lichtenburg Castle in Kusel. Our time off base was precious. I was no longer in Neubrucke, and we missed seeing each other every day. Our travels gave us quality time together. It also allowed us to experience and absorb Germany, its culture and people.

Looking back to 1966, it seems amazing that we saw and

experienced so much in those twelve months. We enjoyed what was happening between us, and we continued to discover more about each other as we drew closer with each day we spent together.

CHAPTER EIGHTEEN

PROMOTIONS

September 1966 My one year anniversary with Special Services came in September. I was still at Neubrucke. That surprised me, as Monti P. my Club Director at Neubrucke was transferred after only ten months. She actually arrived at 98th General Hospital after I did. It was inevitable that I would soon be going to another Club. That meant leaving Pat. I just hoped my new assignment wasn't too far from Neubrucke. Our relationship was too important to let distance make a difference.

Although there was never a word said about my relationship with Pat from my immediate supervisor or the area director, we lived in fear that we would be separated for that reason alone.

After all, dating any of the enlisted men was frowned upon. Dating a colored enlisted man was an even worse transgression. Admittedly, my relationship with Monti was not a good one. Letters to my father revealed that we had as little contact as possible. It helped that we often worked alone. We never socialized outside of work. A request for a promotion would have to come from her. As we disliked each other, I wasn't surprised that I hadn't been transferred with a promotion before my year anniversary. I knew I was good at my job.

When my transfer did come through, I was assigned to the Service Club in Mainz, Germany. The guys there were very different from the G.I.s at 98th General Hospital. Theirs was an air borne unit, and they were rough and ready. So rough in fact that a military policeman (M.P.) was assigned to the pool room. The Service Club girls didn't go in there. What a change!

I was still an NGS 6 and a Program Director at Mainz. My new Club Director, Louise, was a jewel. After only a month on the job, she wrote me an excellent evaluation and recommended a promotion. By the first of December, the promotion came through along with a transfer to Bad Krauznach, Germany, where as an NGS 7, I was the Assistant Club Director. I had only been at Bad Krauznach a short time when the Club Director went on leave back to the States. I became Acting Club Director of a club that was the largest in our district. It was actually our headquarters club. Quite a step up from Neubrucke, the smallest club!

Sara, playing board games, Circa, 1966

Bad Krauznach was supposed to have five full-time Service Club girls. When I was there, it only had three. The club was two stories. It had a craft room, an auditorium with a large stage, a library, a full size kitchen and several card rooms, in addition to the usual pool room, photo lab and music rooms. I was so busy there during the time I was acting director that Pat and I weren't able to do any extensive traveling together. We did talk on the phone every day. Calls between military bases were free. When I was working weekends, Pat drove over to spend the weekend with me. I drove to Neubrucke when I had days off. Bad Krauznach was closer to Neubrucke than Mainz. We burned up the roads going back and forth.

Still it wasn't the same as when we were together every day. It is impossible to describe the thrill, the longing, the joy that wells up inside when two people love each other and become one. Not just on a sensual level, but intellectually. Pat and I shared so much. We thought alike, we anticipated each others words, and we were drawn to the same people. It was if we were joined together. A bond that only grew stronger despite the distance separating us.

While I was busy running the Service Club in Bad Krauznach, Pat was going through the yearly Inspector General inspection at 98th General Hospital. He was also promoted from an E-5 Sergeant to E-6 Staff Sergeant. In a letter to my father, I explained what that promotion meant. "The promotion means more than just money. Pat can now move into a private room (he has had four roommates). He no longer has to get up for reveille at 5:30 every morning. He doesn't have to sign out every time he leaves the barracks, and he doesn't have to take part in GI parties (that means scrubbing walls, waxing floors and cleaning the latrine). As you can see, the jump from E-5 to E-6 is an important one in the Army. It's one of the hardest promotions to get. When you reach E-6, the Army the same as says 'You are a responsible person, and we no longer have to control your every move. You have proved your leadership and ability to handle your job so we guess you can handle your personal life too.' Pat is one of the most responsible, mature people I know, and I'm glad he's finally getting free of the confining set of restrictions the Army imposes. Actually, Pat has reached his present rank in record time. He has been in the Army less than five years, and he's had five promotions."

My father knew how important Pat was to me. He was in every letter I sent home, but he didn't know Pat was colored. In July, I wrote, "I so wish you could meet Pat. He's such a wonderful person." In another letter, I wrote "I know you're really going to like Pat. You have so much in common. It's utterly impossible for me to tell you how good he is. You'll just have to meet him and see for yourself."

I was certain that once he met Pat, his being a Negro wouldn't matter. I kept urging my father to come to Germany for a visit. His grandparents had immigrated from Germany in the 1850's. Our letters for months contained possible plans for when he would come and what he would see once here. We thought about Spain or maybe France for long trips. He did eventually make it to Europe, but that's a story for another chapter.

CHAPTER NINETEEN

THE ENGAGEMENT

December 1966 Fifteen months after we met, Pat asked me to marry him. It wasn't a surprise. Our relationship had been moving steadily toward that culmination over the past several months. My answer, of course, was yes. I had been in love with him since that first Paris trip. When he knew I was the one didn't happen that fast. But Christmas 1965, after he had only known me three months, he gave me a exquisite gold bracelet. He told me years later that even then he knew I was special.

Our memories of that proposal fifty years later are not exactly the same. I know it was just before Christmas. That we agree on. I remember it was in my quarters in Bad Krauznach. My version is more romantic, with Pat kneeling before me and slipping a diamond engagement ring on my finger as he asked me to marry him. Pat doesn't remember the kneeling part. His memory is vague on whether it was in Bad Krauznach or Neubrucke. When I visited in Neubrucke, I stayed in the temporary transit quarters. It made more sense that he popped the question in my own living room in Bad Krauznach. Pat, who can remember minute details of our travels in 1966, admits memories of his proposal are hazy.

When I was transferred to a new Service Club and we were separated, Pat realized just how much he missed me. He missed our daily interaction and closeness. He missed holding hands and sharing our day's happenings. Talking on the phone wasn't the same. He began to think seriously about us spending our lives together beyond Germany.

He had brought a diamond ring with him to Europe. At that time, he had thoughts of asking Vicki, a WAC he had dated at Ft. Leavenworth, Kansas, to marry him. She was still in the Army and stationed in Germany. Arriving in Heidelberg, he discovered she was involved with someone else, so the ring was put aside. Now he got it out and took it to Idar-Oberstein to be reset. Herr Hosser, who worked in the treasurers office at the hospital had been a jeweler until an accident to his hand. He knew everyone in the jewelry industry in Idar-Oberstein. He had taken Pat to his home there and introduced him to the jeweler who made the gold bracelet I received for Christmas 1965. The town was full of talented men who made fine jewelry. When it came time to get the diamond reset, Pat once again turned to Herr Hosser for advice. This time, a different jeweler who worked with diamonds was chosen. The ring had belonged originally to a distant relative of his mother. It was in her possession at the time Pat left for Germany. She gave it to Pat hoping that he would soon give her a daughter-in-law.

Pat designed the new setting. The diamond was set up on four prongs that showed it off to advantage. The setting was white gold. At the same time, Pat ordered wedding bands, also of white gold. He must have been sure of my response to his proposal. He originally wanted plain bands, but the jeweler convinced him to make them more distinctive. The final rings were concave with a design hammered into the gold. Nothing plain there. They were lovely and unique. Our initials were carved inside, mine in his ring and his in mine. Of course, I didn't see the rings until our wedding day at the chapel in Neubrucke on June 17, 1967. But I loved my engagement ring.

Pat and I made a tape recording to announce our engagement to my father. He had written a letter to his mother telling her he was thinking of getting married. How much he told her about me during the past fifteen months was unclear. He was not a letter writer like me. I also wrote a letter to my father enclosing a picture of Pat. Although I had sent many pictures to my father, I have no recollection of ever telling him Pat was a Negro or of sending him a picture of Pat. Both the letter and the tape made it clear that Pat was colored. We could do nothing but await the reactions of both our families to our engagement. Two of Pat's first cousins had already married white partners. My conservative Midwestern family had never known any mixed race unions. What would their reaction be?

CHAPTER TWENTY

THE REACTION

January 1967 My mother passed away unexpectedly when I was twenty. She was a warm, loving woman. When my twenty-one-year-old brother eloped and brought his nineteen-year-old bride home, my mother took them in. She created a comfortable living space for them in our upstairs room. She arranged for a reception to introduce the newlyweds to our friends and relatives. There was never a word of criticism or a sign that she disapproved. As I awaited my father's reaction to our engagement, I longed for my mother's warmth and understanding. My father was a staid, strict German who seldom showed his emotions. He was also a very intelligent, steady man who went out of his way to help others. I loved him dearly and hoped that he would accept my decision to marry Pat.

In the letter announcing my engagement to Pat, I had made it clear he was a Negro. I also hedged and said he was part white on his mother's side, and possibly had American Indian blood on his father's side. Was I trying to make our engagement easier to swallow or just hoping that those closest to me might not reject us if he was part white? The letter and the tape we sent arrived in Ohio, just before Christmas. My father was there visiting my brother and his wife. I wanted them to listen to the tape together.

Christmas had always been a sad time since my mother passed away on December 18. Her presents had been wrapped and under the tree. The big family dinner was to have been at our house. Even six years later, I longed to be with my family for Christmas. It was the hardest time of year for me. I was hoping that my announcement would take away some of the sadness we usually felt as Christmas approached. I didn't expect leaps of joy that I was finally getting married, but I did hope for some words of approval. As Pat and I awaited my father's reply, we tried to go about our usual holiday activities as if our whole future wasn't in limbo.

It took almost a month for my father's response to arrive in Germany. While I was busy at the Service Club and spending as much time as possible with Pat, I was having trouble sleeping at night and was more irritable during the day. Each day that passed without a response brought more angst. I began to doubt that it would be a positive one.

Pat also had a tense time. He was aware that some of his friends didn't approve of our engagement. It wasn't that he was having second thoughts, but he was beginning to realize all the possible roadblocks we could face in our marriage. He was at 98th General Hospital and I was at Bad Kreuznach Service Club fifty miles away. Distance kept us from comforting each other face to face when doubts filtered through our determination and love for each other. In the times we had together, we had serious discussions about all the situations that might occur if we married. We felt prepared to handle whatever came our way.

When I visited Pat at Neubrucke, those who disapproved didn't let their feeling be known to me. Pat was the one who took the brunt of their unfavorable reactions, and in some cases, downright condemnation. To his credit, he never let me see how that affected him. Eventually, just before our wedding in June, he ended up in the hospital with dangerously high blood pressure. Probably a combination of the disapproval he was dealing with from some of his friends and the stress that was building as we confronted a series of problems planning our wedding. Fortunately, his hospital stay was short and his blood pressure brought under control.

When my father's response arrived, his reaction was contradictory. "I consider the Negro a human being and a child of

God the same as myself," he wrote. But, he stated his concern was for the welfare and happiness of both of us. Then he expressed worry that we had not thought things through and shouldn't rush into marriage While I had hoped for a positive reaction to our engagement, what I got was telling me to come home to get married and not to rush into things. To me, that was a rejection of my ability to make my own decisions. I must have read his letter two or three times, trying to find a sentence that I could take as his approval. It wasn't there.

My time with Special Services ended in September 1967. Our original plans were to marry in September so I could remain in Germany until Pat's enlistment was over in January 1968. Four short months. My father advised me to return home in September and take the time to make sure marriage was what I wanted. "I would very much like to talk this over with you," he wrote. Oh, how I would have liked to talk face to face with him. But again, distance was our enemy.

He ended his letter asking that I write to Rev. and Mrs. L.A. Warren and hear what they had to say that would help me "understand the full impact of all aspects concerning your anticipated marriage." I later learned that he drove up to Nebraska to talk with the Warrens himself and inform them of my engagement. I wrote the Warrens. Rev. Warren was the minister who baptized me. He and his wife were my godparents. While they lived in Nebraska, my father visited them often. They fished together in Minnesota every summer. Rev. Warren came from Nebraska to do my mother's funeral. Our families had always been close.

The response I received from Uncle Leland and Aunt Ada, as I always called them, only confused me more. Uncle Leland actually wrote me two letters enclosed in the same envelope. One said, “READ THIS FIRST.” In it, he said he wanted to tear up the second letter and throw it in the wastebasket. He wrote, “All I really want to do is open my arms to both you and Pat and take you into some better culture where there are no problems and where all right-thinking people could live together in peace and love.”

BUT! “Because you are dear to us, there must be no compromising in the frankness of what I must write to you in answer to your letter of January 22.” That second letter was long – three typed pages single-spaced. He addressed four issues in depth. First, did we understand that living in a city would not shield us from prejudice? He had lived and taught in Harlem and understood city prejudices well. Second, my statement that the opinion of only a half-dozen people was all that mattered to me might well be regretted down the road. He felt I tossed off too lightly the impact of what blood relationships would mean to me as I grew older. Third, he pointed out that my actions and decisions did not take place in a social vacuum. My father, brother and all other relatives and friends shared the problem with me. I was forcing others to face my problems whether or not they desired to do so. Fourth, had we considered the critical issue of children? Were we willing to bring children into the world who would have to labor against belonging to both, but actually to neither race?

While Uncle Leland brought up legitimate concerns, they were all things Pat and I had discussed at length. Of course, there would be problems. What my father and the Warrens thought were problems were things that we knew we could handle. They would be problems for those who had prejudices, not for us. It was their problem, not ours. We never thought that love was a problem.

In the end, Uncle Leland advised that I come home in September as my father wanted and take the time to make sure of my decision. He acknowledged there were laws in some states that prohibited marriages between different races. I should come home and make my own explanations to family and friends. I learned later that my father was with the Warrens when that letter was written. Uncle Leland read it to him. Had I followed their advice, my incredible marriage to an incredible man might never have happened.

While we were disappointed in the response we received, we remained steadfast in our decision to marry later that year. Missouri was one of the states that had anti-miscegenation laws. I'm not sure if my father realized that. He did know such laws existed, as Uncle Leland had mentioned them in his letter. It would have been impossible for us to be married in my hometown among family and friends.

A wedding in Germany among our friends there was the alternative choice. We hoped my father and Pat's mother would come to Europe for the wedding.

Civil Rights unrest was still very much a part of the scene in the United States in 1967. The assassination of Dr. Martin Luther King in 1968 led to more militant leaders in the Civil Rights movement. Peaceful marches often turned violent. Truthfully, Pat and I didn't follow what was happening in the States that closely. As we set the date for our wedding and began to make plans, we were much too involved in our own situation to pay attention to what was happening thousands of miles away.

We still hadn't heard from my brother, Robert, Pat's mother or my aunt, Edythe Kelly who had all been informed of our engagement. Their reactions could be similar to my father's. Chances are they would be the same or worse. As 1967 started, our love and commitment remained strong.

CHAPTER TWENTY-ONE

THE REACTION CONTINUED

February 1967 Once my father returned home after Christmas he wrote that I "should forget about Robert." He told me he had discussed my engagement with my brother during the holidays. He would, however, expect Robert to tell me himself what his reaction was. The furthest my father would go was the "forget" advice. That was enough to alert me as to what was to come.

In preparation for writing my memoir, I had located all the correspondence between my family and friends that spanned the years 1965 through 1968. The letters were stored in shoeboxes on the top shelf of the bedroom closet. On Sunday, October 4, 2015, at 7:30 p.m., I sat down on the couch in my home office with the

1967 box of letters in my lap. I was finally ready to write seriously about what occurred in my family when I announced my engagement to a black man. I had already counted the letters. There were 77 covering the year 1967. I put them in chronological order. Admittedly, a delaying tactic. I wasn't sure I wanted to go back to those stressful times forty-eight years earlier.

I knew I had received a letter from Robert, but it wasn't in the box. I looked again, but no letter. Even without the letter, I remember what he said. The letter was short and said, "I feel you have made a mistake, and I do not want to be any part of that mistake." My response was even shorter. "Communication received and noted. Auf Wiedersehn." That was the only time I heard from my brother in nine years. No birthday or Christmas cards. No letters or phone calls. Family gatherings, funerals, marriages and births all passed without any word from my brother. It was passive avoidance on both our sides. I did as my father said and forgot about him.

I never asked my father about my brother in any of my letters or phone calls. My father's letters, however, included the latest news of what my brother and his wife were doing. It's difficult to forget about someone when you are constantly given information of their doings. I'm sure our father relayed news about me in the letters he wrote my brother. In more than one letter, he mentioned that Robert asked about me. During those nine years of silence between my brother and I, my father must have felt the need to act as a go-between in hopes there would be a reconciliation. I had put my father in that awkward position. Uncle Leland had warned me that would happen.

Was I devastated by Robert's rejection? No. The main emotion was sadness. We had never been close. I was the needy one in our relationship. In high school and college, I longed for him to play the protective, big brother role, but he never did. He wasn't there to ward off the teasing. He didn't make sure I was safe on all the many bus trips we took with the high school band. He didn't compliment me on my accomplishments. Why would I expect him to support me in this situation?

My brother was adopted. As so often happens, I came along six months later. Unfortunately, I always felt Robert thought I was the favorite. Our parents had tried for nine years to have a baby. Although they treated us equally with love and support, looking back now, I feel he was insecure. We were a study in contrasts. I was shy – he was outgoing. I was studious – he was fun loving. I taught dance in my own studio – he worked on our relatives' farms. I obeyed all the rules – he snuck in after curfew.

Once we were adults and were leading our own lives in different states, our relationship changed little. Our contacts were infrequent and centered mostly around our concern for our widowed, aging father. Robert was married and had a successful career in education. There was no one around to compare him to his sister. In a town as small as Oregon, Missouri, it was inevitable that comparisons were made. I got As in high school. Robert passed. I was active in the church and community. Robert enjoyed an active social life. Two very different people. Ironically, I was the one who introduced him to his future wife She was a Delta Zeta sorority sister. I'm sure he was relieved we now lived hundreds of miles apart. He moved to Ohio, his wife's home state. After earning his master's degree, he became a principal in the Massillon, Ohio, school system. Later he moved to Shaker Heights as an assistant superintendent. There is a newspaper article from the local paper in Oregon announcing the fact that brother and sister, Robert and Sara Beth Kurtz, received their master's degrees on the same day (see photo, end of chapter). When that happened in 1965, there was no divide between the two of us. But it would appear that we were still subconsciously competing with each other.

It's not surprising that reactions to our engagement were not positive and supportive. The social unrest in the South was spreading to other parts of the country. Prejudices that had been suppressed for years sprang forth with the advancement of the Civil Rights movement. At one time, forty-one states had anti-miscegenation laws prohibiting marriage or sexual relations between a man and woman of different races. Gradually, states repealed those laws until in 1967, only sixteen states remained. It was a time of unrest, but also a time of progress. Jim Crow laws no longer ruled in the South. Schools were being integrated successfully. In contrast George Wallace, in 1963, had personally blocked integration of the University of Alabama when he stood in the doorway refusing to allow two black students to enter. The summer of 1967 would prove to be a violent one, with race riots in places like Detroit and Watts. Knowing the climate of the country in 1967, the safety of any mixed race couple would be at risk. Looking back, I can understand the concerns of my family.

Pat's mother was the one person who had no opposition to our engagement. His family already had two mixed marriages. Today, Pat believes she was relieved he was finally getting married. As soon as we set the wedding day, she began her plans to come to Germany for the wedding. She also ordered wedding announcements to be printed. My father would not be at the wedding, not because he disapproved of our marriage, but because June was one of the busiest times on the farm. His brothers relied on his help. He had accepted the fact that I would not be coming home, but would be married in Germany.

We still hadn't heard from my aunt, Edythe Kelly. She was the widow of my mother's brother and lived in New Jersey. Returning to my shoebox full of 1967 letters, I bundled them by writer. There were letters from her to me, plus her letters to my father. It was a week after I had read the letters from my father and the Warrens. It was hot. Too hot for October. I closed the blinds in my home office and turned on my little one speed fan. Dust motes floated lazily in the bands of sun that escaped through the blinds. It was time to reread the letters I had received from Aunt Edythe. I had never read those she wrote to my father. They, along with all the other letters my father had received and saved, were rescued when he passed away. They had been stored but not read. I had started to read them when I started writing this memoir. They were a treasure trove of information and brought back memories of things I had long forgotten.

As I tried to remove the old rubber band around Aunt Edythe's letters, it snapped, causing the letters to spread out on my lap. The band itself flew back into the shoebox. There hadn't been any noise, but the breaking of the band startled me. Later, I would remember that silent break. The information I gleaned from her letters to my father startled me just as much as the snapping rubber band had. The letters she had written to me had no condemnation or criticism. So I was completely unprepared for what I found in the letters she wrote my father. The letter dated February 26 was the first of four she wrote to him in one month. "What baffles me most is how the mixed friendship started. There had to be something in her social life that brought about this Joan of Arc crusade."

I sat on the couch with the letter in my lap. My eyes were closed, but my mind was busy trying to reconcile what I had read with what I had always believed. Believe me, there was nothing wrong with my social life in Germany. I had written at length about the people and events of the past year to both my father and Aunt Edythe. There had been many opportunities to develop a relationship with men I had met, but I chose Pat. Nothing Joan of Arc about it. I wasn't trying to single-handedly solve the problem of prejudice. I simply and irrevocably was attracted and fell in love.

In a second letter she wrote, “All members of my family seem to be on one great bender! I do not mean drunk.” Her niece was engaged to a Negro, her granddaughter's baby would arrive just six months after her wedding and her nephew was divorcing his third wife. I tried to tell myself that her reaction to my announcement was just part of her coping with a barrage of startling news. What bothered me most was her saying that she was “silenced” by her family's behavior. She could no longer talk about us with her friends and neighbors. We had embarrassed her by our actions.

In 1967, I didn't call her Aunt Edythe. After her husband (Homer Blaine Kelly) died in 1952, she started going by the single name Kelly. That is how she signed all our correspondence. Her only daughter died in a choking accident in a restaurant before anyone had heard of the Heimlich maneuver. When I lost my mother at age 20, she reached out to me. Though she lived in New Jersey and I in Missouri, we were brought together by a shared need. She became my second mother. I became her second daughter. Ironically, before my mother's death, I had only met Kelly twice. The first time was on the family trip to visit my aunt and uncle when I was seven years old. Remember the Rockettes and Radio City Music Hall? Then in 1958, when I was on the Mission Study Tour, we were able to meet for a short time when the tour stopped in New Jersey. She drove over, and we tried to squeeze getting to know each other into that brief visit.

After my mother died we met again on two occasions. As a college graduation present, she sent me a round trip plane ticket to come visit her. She also gave me a beautiful diamond and sapphire family ring that she had reset. My daughter received that ring when she graduated from college. The week I spent with her in New Jersey allowed us to actually explore all the things we had written about in our letters. When I was at the University of Wisconsin one summer, she was taking a three-week train excursion through Canada that made a stop in Chicago. As soon as I knew the date, I arranged to meet her at the Palmer House for lunch. Despite only having met four times, we had a special bond.

After my mother's death, we had started to correspond. I wrote her all the things I wished I could tell my mother. Even though I had met Kelly briefly in New Jersey in 1958, I had no visual image of her in my mind. If you asked me for a physical description of her, I didn't have one. She existed on paper. I knew her from her letters. She was practical with a wealth of advice and encouragement to her twenty-year-old niece when we first started to correspond. She had a sense of humor as she told tales of events in her life. She could make her daily meetings with friends at the swimming pool seem like an adventure. She valued family ties and made it clear I was important to her. She made me feel loved. Her influence in my life helped me become the well-rounded person I am today.

Because Kelly was important to me, her reaction to our engagement was crucial. Would she accept or reject? I now knew that in my letters she accepted. In the letters to my father, she disapproved in no uncertain terms. I slipped her letters back into their envelopes and sat quietly, trying to absorb what I had read. It was difficult for me to see the Kelly I had known and loved in those letters to my father. Why had she let me think she had no problems with our engagement but write differently to my father? Was she trying to help him cope with my actions by agreeing with his concerns? She too had written at length about the problems we would be facing once we returned to the States. Her concerns echoed those of both my father and Uncle Leland. I now knew how my family reacted. Not that well.

I didn't reread the letters I received from Kelly in early 1967.

They gave no indication of her true feelings. I slipped a new rubber band around the small stack and put them back in the shoebox. My only consolation was the fact that once Pat and I returned to the States in 1968 and were living in New York, we enjoyed a close relationship with her right up until her death in 1980. I'm glad I didn't know about the things she wrote to my father at that time. I like to think that once she met Pat, she realized I had made a good choice.

Degrees to Brother and Sister

Miss Sara Beth Kurtz and G. Robert Kurtz, daughter and son of Willard I. Kurtz, Oregon, Mo., received their master's degrees on the same day. Miss Kurtz received her degree in physical education from the University of Wisconsin and will become a recreation director with the special services division of the department of the army. She will report to Washington Sept. 13 for orientation prior to an assignment to an army base in Europe.

Mr. Kurtz was awarded a master of education degree from the University of Missouri through the extension division at Northwest Missouri State College, Maryville. He will be principal of the Frazer Elementary School, Massillon, Ohio, where he has been a teacher the last four years. The school provides facilities for neurologically handicapped and mentally retarded children. Prior to going to Ohio, Mr. Kurtz taught in St. Joseph.

The brother and sister are graduates of the college in Maryville.

Newspaper announcement of graduation, 1965.

CHAPTER TWENTY-TWO

COUSINS

I have at least a hundred cousins that I know of. There are probably hundreds more out there somewhere that I don't know about. Most of them stem from my paternal great grandparents, Isaac Kurtz and Mary Seaman Kurtz, who immigrated from Germany in the early 1850's. They came from the same small town: Auggen, Germany. Both Isaac and Mary already had relatives who had come to the States and settled near Oregon, Missouri. We still have relatives in Auggen. Two of my cousins visited them recently.

How well Isaac and Mary knew each other before they immigrated is not known. We do know they were not married when they left Germany. They arrived in the States on the same boat and must have gotten pretty well acquainted on that six-week journey. The family has the ship's manifest with their names on it. Their boat docked in New Orleans. Isaac made his way up the Mississippi River to St. Louis, Missouri, where he ran out of money. He stayed there and worked until he earned enough to move on. Not sure how Mary got to Missouri, but it was also probably via the Mississippi and Missouri Rivers. Oregon is located just a few miles from the banks of the Missouri.

Isaac and Mary married. I like to think their romance started on that long boat ride. They had thirteen children, eleven of them boys. If you look in the Oregon, Missouri, phone book today, there are still more Kurtz's than any other last name. Every class in the Oregon school system had at least one Kurtz. My class had three. Then there's the Markt, Buntz, Feuerbacher, Seaman, Gee, Miller and Noellche families. All relatives. All Germans.

The Kurtzs were farmers. Isaac and Mary and the two daughters lived in the small house on the farm. The eleven boys slept in the barn. That house still stands. It has been added on to, and a family lives in it. There are at least a dozen Kurtz families who are still farmers in and around Oregon, but a Kurtz no longer lives at the original homestead.

At a Kurtz family reunion at the Holt County Fall Festival in Oregon in 2007, there were Kurtzs from all over the country.

Washington, Kansas, Wyoming, Delaware, New York and of course, Missouri. I met some of those hundreds of cousins I didn't even know about. In the big parade at the Festival, the Kurtz entry had almost a dozen vehicles, plus a crop duster plane that flew overhead as they passed the judge's stand. There were pickup trucks, tractor pulled wagons, SUVs and cars of all kinds. My father's first cousin, Helen, who was one hundred years old, led the Kurtz contingent riding in a big SUV. Pat and I rode in that parade. Pat was probably the first black man to ever grace a Fall Festival parade in Oregon. The Kurtzs took the grand prize which meant a trophy and a cash award of one hundred dollars.

On the maternal side my great, great grands came from Ireland in 1806. Their name was Kelly, and they were from protestant northern Ireland near Armagh. They started the crossing to the States with an infant son, James, who died at sea. He is buried in the Atlantic. Their firstborn child in this country was also named James. They had six children. They weren't as prolific as the Kurtz's. Still, I was related to the Ramseys, Kneales, Hibberds, Meyers and Browns. The Kellys worked their way west from New York, with a stop in Ohio before settling in Missouri. Unlike the Kurtzs, the Kellys didn't have a lot of Irish lasses to choose their brides from. My great grandfather, Robert Logan Kelly (the one who died in the Civil War), married a woman of French descent by the name of Cassandra de la Perrigo. My grandfather, James Kelly, married a woman of English descent, Sarah Brimhall. Her ancestors can be traced back to William the Conqueror.

I'm sure all my relatives in Oregon, Missouri, knew I had married a black man long before our first visit in 1968. Word spreads fast in a small town. The announcement of our wedding had appeared in the local paper. No mention there that Pat was black. His real name, Vince C. Aldrich, was used in that announcement. I actually didn't know what to expect when we made that first visit. I'm not exaggerating when I say there was hardly a ripple in the flow of everyday life in Oregon when we arrived. No curious relatives stopping by the house to check us out. No rash of phone calls to see if we were home. No interruption of the daily business of farming, grocery shopping in town on Saturday, going to church on Sunday. There were plenty of friendly hellos and handshakes whenever we were out and about. After church on Sunday, people came up to greet us just as they would any other couple who were visiting from out of town. The people in my hometown appeared to be color blind.

Shortly after our marriage, I received a letter with an enclosed check from Mrs. Glen and Mrs. Hitz, the matriarchs of the Presbyterian Church in Oregon. Well into their seventies, they had lived all their lives in Oregon and were much respected by the townspeople. Mrs. Glen wrote, “My sister, Mrs. Hitz, joins me in wishing you and your husband a very happy life together. Vince is certainly a fortunate man to have such a lovely talented wife. I'm sure he knows how lucky he is." That letter warmed my heart. It would have been perfect if everyone felt the same way. That was certainly not the case.

My mother's cousins who lived in St. Joseph, Missouri made it clear that we were not welcome in their home. That information was received in a letter from Helen H. who was my mother's first cousin once removed. Her mother and my grandmother were first cousins. The result of that letter was eight years of estrangement with her family. I always thought that Helen's husband made that decision. I remembered him as having strong feelings about anyone of another race. What made this more hurtful was that Helen's daughter and I had been close since birth. Sally Ann was eighteen months younger than me and named after me. Her mother once said that Sally Ann was as close as she could get to Sara Beth. Even though we lived thirty miles apart, our families spent many weekends and holidays together as we were growing up.

Losing Sally was more painful than losing my brother. Girls tend to bond more. We went to the same college. She became a teacher. I went on to graduate school. Sally married while I was in Germany. Ironically our married names both start with "A" and are very similar. We each had two children, a son first, followed by a daughter. Our lives seemed to run parallel courses.

Just because I was out of favor, I made it clear to my father that it was important to maintain close ties with Sally's family. They were the closest relatives on my mother's side. I was glad when he continued to visit them regularly. There was never any indication of a strain in their relationship. One of the family traditions that stemmed out of the yearly fishing trips to Minnesota was the big fish fries that happened several times each summer. Sometimes Sally's family hosted, and sometimes my father had everyone at his house in Oregon. Wherever they were held, the whole family gathered for a happy, delicious feast. For years, my father was the official tarter sauce maker. Made from scratch, his tarter sauce was delicious. He should have patented it! I always enjoyed reading about those fish fries in my father's letters. Unlike with my brother, I wanted to hear about what Sally and her family were doing.

One summer when we were in Missouri visiting my father, we went to St. Joseph to shop. Our shopping finished, we were relaxing in the rocking chairs by the fountain in the mall when I saw Sally walk by. Not stopping to think, I ran after her, calling her name. She turned around, and I stopped a few feet from her. We stared at each other. I held my breath. Would she acknowledge me or turn away? Glancing over my shoulder, I saw Pat had followed me. If she accepted me, she would also have to accept him.

It was probably only a matter of seconds, but it seemed like eons before she broke into a smile and said my name. My tension slipped away, and I could breathe again. Sally came from the English side of the family. With my German blood, neither of us was prone to emotional outbursts. There was no hugging, laughing or verbal exclamations. I introduced her to Pat, and we talked for a few minutes. Anyone looking for fireworks would have been disappointed.

I now had part of my family back. Sally and her family were once again in the fold. Sally told me that it was her parents who had rejected us, but they had both passed away. From that day on, our families have been close. During the years when my father suffered from ill health and had to go into a nursing home, it was Sally who visited him and kept me informed. We see them every time we return to Missouri and have stayed in their home many times. No dramatic ending here, just a happy one.

So far prejudice against our marriage had come from only two main sources: my brother and Sally's parents. There were undercurrents of disapproval like Kelly's that we were never aware of. Pat and I agree now that we simply blocked many of the possible outside influences and just went about living our lives the way we wanted. If they didn't approve, it was their problem, not ours.

CHAPTER TWENTY-THREE

WEST BERLIN

February 1967 By February, Pat and I realized we both needed a rest. As Acting Club Director at Bad Krauznach while the Club Director was in the States, I had survived a European-wide Drama Convention, followed by the annual Command Inspection from Special Services Headquarters. I was able to salvage something of the Service Club from the rubble left by the convention so the inspecting team had something to inspect. We did fine.

Pat's situation was similar. His supervisor was having surgery, leaving Pat in charge of the entire Registrar Section of the hospital. The section had lost three men through normal rotations with no replacements. The hospital also had their Command Inspection.

Not only was Pat in charge of the Registrar Section for the inspection, he was also Barrack's Sergeant and responsible for getting the living quarters ready for the inspection. There were no problems with either of our inspections, but the stress added to the anxiety about the reaction to our engagement had taken its toll.

We decided to relax for a week without thinking about our jobs, the Army, our families or our future. That week was spent in Berlin, Germany. Why did we choose Berlin? I remember Pat saying he had talked to several guys who were stationed there. All said it was a must see. I doubt if they were concerned about the political or historic situation in Berlin. In 1967, the city was thriving culturally and economically. I'm talking about West Berlin. East Berlin was a completely different story.

Berlin became two cities after World War II. The Allies acquired West Berlin. The Soviets gained control of East Berlin. West Berlin was technically an occupied city with France, Great Britain and the United States each having a sector. The Soviets cutting off all overland access into West Berlin led to the historic Berlin Airlift during Truman's administration in 1948 and 1949. Two million tons of food were flown into the city on 270,000 flights. It was a resounding success for the Allies. The Soviets eventually admitted defeat. Military trains and vehicles were once again able to move in and out of the city bringing in supplies and personnel. They were subject, of course, to restrictions and inspections.

Berlin was completely surrounded by East Germany. It wasn't until 1970 that a treaty allowed civilian trains and cars to cross East Germany to get to the city.

By 1960, one thousand East Berliners a day were leaving for West Berlin. A massive exodus. To stop this flow, in 1961, the Soviets built the Berlin Wall. JFK made his famous “Ich ben ein Berliner” speech at the Rathaus Schoneberg in February 1963. Four years later, Pat and I were able to experience both East and West Berlin on a trip arranged through the U.S. Army. While we would enjoy the culture and excitement of West Berlin, there would be a serious side to our trip. The contrast between East and West was evident in the two sides of Berlin. The Cold War was heating up. Pat and I needed to see both sides and get a feeling for how the future might play out.

Leaving on the troop train from Frankfurt, Germany at 8:00 p.m., crossing into East Germany at 4:00 a.m., and arriving in West Berlin four hours later, we were eager to explore what had been described to us as a very cosmopolitan city. Pat had to wear his uniform on the troop train. When we crossed into East Germany, Soviet soldiers boarded the train to check everyone's papers. Trying to be as inconspicuous as possible, I handed over my passport and military pass. At 4:00 a.m., most of us were half asleep. The engine was switched for an East German one. All the window shades had to be pulled down so we could not look out and see any of East Germany. I wonder what they were hiding? It was dark out anyway. I'm sure the thousands of stars overhead were the same for the East and the West. Once we arrived in Allied territory, the engine was switched again. It was a long and tiring night.

When we finally got to our hotel in the American sector, we actually slept for a couple of hours before going out to explore. In a ten-page letter to my father, I described our visit. Following a guided tour of the city, I wrote, "Berlin is trying just a little too hard to appear gay, modern and progressive. There is almost a carnival atmosphere on the surface, but underneath, it is a sad city, one that is hurt to the core by the cruel wall that cuts through its center."

The more of Berlin we saw, the more we wished we could have seen it before the war. We felt it would have rivaled Paris for it's beauty and magnificence. The Kurfustendamn with its luxurious stores reminded us of the Champs-Elysees. The bombed-out Kaiser Wilhelm Church at the end of the street was a stark reminder of the war. It was the only ruined building that remained in the Allied sector. Actually, only the bell tower was a ruin. The main body of the church was completely rebuilt and very modern. The Dahlem Museum, with the largest collection of Rembrandt paintings in the world, also housed the 3,300-year-old limestone bust of the

Egyptian Queen Nefertiti. Its colors still vibrant, it was exquisite. The Kempinski Restaurant on the Kurfustendamn provided us with several excellent meals. I was never a fan of lamb chops, but those served at the Kempinski were almost like the Weiner Schnitzel (breaded veal cutlets) I loved.

I experienced my first opera when we saw *La Boheme*. Pat began listening to The New York Metropolitan Opera's Saturday radio program with his father when he was ten years old. He could tell you, in Italian, the name of every aria from *La Boheme*. My Midwest musical taste was for the operettas of Sigmund Romberg, especially *The Desert Song* and *The Student Prince*. Knowing nothing about opera, when I wrote to my father, I concentrated on the setting and not the music. "The opera house is a new building and nothing was spared to make it modern and technically perfect. The stage revolves and is so huge an opera with twenty-five different scenes can be handled with ease.

"During the half-hour intermission, champagne was served in the lounge area. We saw people in evening clothes mixing with people in more casual dress. What really destroyed the whole image, however, was seeing an elegant lady in a floor length gown gulping down a huge bratwurst that was at least a foot long. Bratwurst in one hand and champagne in the other."

The Unter den Linden (under the linden trees) is a beautiful avenue running East-West through Berlin. The trees were planted in 1647 in the grassed pedestrian mall in the middle of the street. In the 19th century, the Unter den Linden was the grandest, best known street in Berlin. During the construction of the North-South tunnel in 1934 and 1935, many of the trees were destroyed. Hitler put Nazi flags on all the trees but eventually took them down when the people protested vigorously. At the end of World War II, the rest were either destroyed by the bombing or cut down for firewood. Fortunately, the trees were replaced in 1950. By the time we saw them, the avenue was once again under the linden trees. Many of the classical buildings lining the street on the West side had been restored. Every effort had been made to bring West Berlin back to its prewar glory, but it was still only half a city.

During the guided tour the first day, great emphasis was placed on the wall. The only word to adequately describe it is ugly. It was dark and rough, and the barbed wire on the top added to the feeling of isolation you got when looking at it. The long stretch of bare dirt leading from the foot of the wall on the west side to where normal life began again in a vibrant, modern city made you aware you were looking at the contrast between progression and regression. I had a strong desire to see that regression on the other side. A feeling of sadness seemed to emanate from the very starkness of the structure. Many lives were lost as people tried to escape by scaling the wall. Government officials finally opened the wall so people could travel between the two Berlins in 1989. The actual destruction of the wall started on June 13, 1990, and was completed in 1992. How ironic, that the start of the wall's demise began on our twenty-third wedding anniversary.

West Berlin gave us a picture of what could be accomplished in just twenty-two short years to build up a modern city from the rubble of war. It was bright and shining, business was flourishing, the people were thriving. Yet underneath it all was a sadness and a longing to be whole again.

CHAPTER TWENTY-FOUR

EAST BERLIN

February 1967 Our tour of East Berlin was taken the day after the tour of the Western sector. That way we were able to make a comparison while both were fresh in our minds. In East Berlin, there was no freedom of speech, you couldn't own land, prices were high and everyone was paid the same salary. The factory worker made the same as the college professor. The firefighter earned what the janitor did. There were no unions or right to work laws. Travel outside the city was restricted. The wall separated parents and children. In many cases, grandchildren had never seen grandparents who lived only a few miles away. This information was certainly not part of the tour. I had done my research before we left for Berlin.

All my senses were on alert the day of our East Berlin tour. A cool breeze had greeted us as we left our hotel early that morning. The bright sun kept it from being too cold. Pat was once again in uniform. With the sharp crease in his pants and his erect military posture, he looked ready to face down the Soviets and protect me from whatever danger there might be. For once, Pat was without his camera. No picture taking was allowed on the tour. While people took these tours every day, my self-protective instincts told me not to call attention to ourselves or ask too many questions. I had visions of us being pulled off the bus and interrogated! Thank goodness my imaginings were just that. We knew, however, that incidents did happen. We were told at the beginning of the tour not to stray from the group, to keep up and stay together. I'm sure there were times when stragglers might have been picked up by the police. Actually, most of the tour time was spent on the bus. The East German authorities didn't want us wandering around on our own. With Pat at my side, I was no longer nervous or afraid.

As our bus approached Check Point Charlie, there was none of the excited chatter you usually find with tourists. The atmosphere was somber as we weaved in and out between the low concrete barriers that led up to the gate. We could see the sun's glare reflecting off the guns of the soldiers who stood watch in the guard towers a few feet beyond the gate. As a soldier examined our papers, a mirror was moved back and forth under the bus to make sure no one was clinging to the undercarriage. Why, I thought, would anyone want to sneak into East Berlin? Shouldn't they be worried about someone trying to get out when we came back across? I learned later that they weren't just looking for people, but bombs, packages, even letters. With no legal communication between families separated by the wall, people resorted to all kinds of desperate ways to keep in touch.

Once through Check Point Charlie, we could see the area of bare dirt on this side was much wider than in the West. The manned guard towers were strategically stationed as far as the eye could see. Coiled barbed wire stretched along the dirt, like tumbleweeds in the desert. This was *No Man's Land.* The sight of those guard towers with armed soldiers brought home why so many people had failed in their attempts to escape to the West.

The bus stopped, and our guide joined us. He was a student at Humboldt University and spoke excellent English. I'm not sure I would have recognized propaganda if I heard it. He seemed to be factual. Much of what he related was historical in nature. Most of the government buildings, cathedrals and palaces that were bombed during the war were in the Eastern sector. In writing to my father, I explained why the city had left them in ruins twenty-two years after the war: "The cost of restoring them to their original beauty is prohibitive. One building would probably run well over ten million dollars, and there must be at least twenty such buildings. Instead of tearing them down, the Communists have left them as they are so people can still come and see them and be awed by their magnificence. Even in their ruined, bombed out condition, they are still beautiful and have historical significance." That was the reason given by the guide. Was it propaganda? I had to admit you could see how magnificent the buildings had been, but I definitely wasn't awed by their bombed out state. Instead I was saddened. Personally, I thought the Soviets just didn't want to spend the money.

Cars seemed to be plentiful, although there were far more bicycles than cars. Construction was going on everywhere. There was a depressing sameness about all the new buildings that had gone up.

In my father's letter, I wrote, "They are mainly prefabricated apartment buildings, and they all look alike: rather drab and unimaginative. Their public buildings, too, are stark and plain. Every corner has a guard house where armed East German police stand watch. What they're watching for I'm not sure, but their presence makes one uneasy. We saw no residential areas where there were private homes. Private homes are not a part of a Communist society so none have grown up in East Berlin. Everyone lives in the prefabricated apartments mentioned earlier."

We made a stop at one of those buildings and were given a tour of an apartment. Although nothing was said about all the apartments being the same, I doubt if there was any diversity except perhaps for the number of bedrooms to accommodate large families. It was apparent that the apartment we saw was just for show. The furnishings were utilitarian. No pictures, books or vases of flowers. Nothing of a personal nature. Individualism is not part of a Communist society. The people who served us refreshments in the lobby spoke English and were friendly but reserved. Direct answers to questions were avoided if they touched on a controversial topic such as how much it cost to live in the building. By this time, everyone on the tour realized that there would be no answers to any questions that might put the Soviets in a bad light.

There was only one other stop where we were allowed off the bus. It was evident that what we were seeing was carefully planned by the government. The second stop was at the Soviet World War II Memorial located in the gardens of Treptower Park. Over twenty thousand Soviet soldiers perished during the Battle of Berlin in 1945. Seven thousand of them are buried at the Memorial. Striking in its simplicity, it was built with stones and granite from the demolished New Reich Chancellery. It was here that we both wished we had our cameras. Approaching the portal, we passed between a towering pair of stylized Soviet flags built of red granite. At the base of each is a kneeling soldier. The large open space between the entrance and the mausoleum at the other end is lined on either side with large sarcophagi. Each is decorated with friezes of war scenes. Atop the mausoleum, reached by an impressive set of stairs, is a twelve-foot statue of a Soviet soldier with a sword holding a German child and standing over a broken swastika. There was a feeling of sadness for all the lives that were lost. I actually had a chill and goose bumps as I gazed at the kneeling soldier statues. Coming away, I thought that in this one thing, the Soviets had gotten it right. That memorial was the single most impressive thing we saw that day. Once again, we had to stay together as a group and couldn't wander around on our own. We wished we could have spent more time at the memorial, but were soon rushed back to the bus. I was to remember that statue and the broken swastika whenever I thought of our trip to Berlin.

I had a profound sense of relief as we passed back through Check Point Charlie and were once again on free ground. Looking back at the wall, I wondered how the people of West Berlin could stand to see it every day. Then again, I thought how much more devastating it was for the East Berliners. It was the symbol of all they had lost.

As our time in Berlin drew to a close, we had one last dinner at our favorite cafe. We talked about the contrast of what we had experienced in the two Berlins. We would soon board the troop train for our trip home. This time, we knew what to expect as we crossed from East to West. This time, the soldiers seemed even more sinister as we knew exactly what they represented. This time, we were appreciative of the freedom we had taken for granted before.

Looking back on that visit almost fifty years ago, I realize that while we were aware that we were witnessing history, it didn't sink in just how important the story of East versus West was. We saw two completely different ways of life in a city that longed to come together again. I thought the German people were victims not only of Hitler, but of those who divided up the spoils of war.

CHAPTER TWENTY-FIVE

PAT'S STORY

Pat has been right beside me since we met in September 1965. Now it's time to tell his story. These are the facts. No sugar coating.

Pat was a mistake. His parents, Vince Collier Aldrich and Carol Thurber Aldrich, were domestics. Employed by Everett Meeks, Dean of the Fine Arts School at Yale University, Vince was the valet/chauffeur. Carol was the housekeeper/cook. They lived in. Dean Meeks' apartment on campus was large and luxurious, but a bachelor's pad was no place for children.

Vince and Carol were living in a world that gave them a status most Negro families in New Haven, Connecticut, couldn't even imagine. Dean Meeks entertained often, and Vince and Carol rubbed shoulders with many important academics and luminaries in the art world. Carol bought her groceries at the most expensive market. Vince bought his clothes at Rogers Peet. They were used to the finer things in life. Their status was defined by the status of their employer.

It was a lifestyle that suited them, and there was no thought of having a family. Having a child would alter everything about their lives. And things did change one June, when they went to a family wedding in Brooklyn. A little too much to drink and the romance of a wedding made them less cautious than usual. Carol found herself with child. Their lives would never be the same. A decision had to be made.

They considered all the possible options, even abortion which was illegal. They could live out instead of in at Dean Meek's apartment, but that didn't suit the Dean. He wanted his employees on hand at all times. A confirmed bachelor, he didn't want to welcome a baby into his private world. There was always adoption, but Carol especially didn't like that idea. Like most expectant mothers, she felt a bond with her unborn child. The only solution they could agree on was to put the baby in a foster home but maintain contact. Pat was four months old when he went to live with the Jordan family in Hamden, Connecticut.

Vince Collier Aldrich, Jr. was born on St. Patrick's Day 1936 in Brooklyn, New York. That was where Carol's family lived, and she went home to have her baby. Vince Sr. stayed behind and took care of Dean Meeks. He was an excellent cook, and before he met Carol, he had done all the cooking. Because of his St. Patrick's Day birthday, Vince, Jr. was nicknamed Pat. That name stuck with him all his life. His maternal grandfather's name was Henry. Thank goodness that name wasn't chosen. Henry Aldrich was the name of a comic character on a popular radio show of the time.

There are two stories about how he was first called Pat. Pat's mother, Carol, told it this way: He was born in a Catholic hospital with a Jewish doctor. The nurse who first brought him in to his mother was also Catholic. As she handed the newborn to Carol, she said “Here's your little St. Patrick.” Pat's father's version has different characters but with the same results. Vince Collier Aldrich, Sr. proudly took his new son in to show him to some of his friends at Yale University. One of the Irish guards commented when he saw the baby, “You have a little St. Patrick.” Absolutely nobody called him Vince, Vinnie, or Junior. I didn't know his real name until just before we got married!

The Jordans were a middle-class Negro family. The father worked for the post office. The mother occasionally worked as a maid for a family in Hamden doing cleaning and laundry. There were two children in the family, a boy and a girl, both much older than baby Pat. Vince and Carol paid the family to care for Pat, and on their days off, they spent time with him. As he grew older, he was allowed into their lives more. He remembers visiting his parents in Dean Meeks' apartment. The Dean was a short, portly man with a Van Dyck beard and a mustache. He allowed Pat to use his old Remington typewriter. Pat typed the names of all the states and their capitols. Even as a young child he was precocious. He was reading by the time he was four.

Pat may not have had any brothers or sisters, but he did have seven first cousins. One was older, and two were younger. The other four were close to Pat in age, and they grew up with a bond that made them feel like siblings. All were children of his mother's four sisters.

Dean Meeks owned a summer home in Old Lyme, Connecticut. It was on an inlet off the Long Island Sound. As Pat got older, Vince and Carol would bring him with them when they spent weekends there. Pat has good memories of those times in Old Lyme. He remembers going crabbing with his mother and the delicious crab cakes and crab salad she made from their catch. He loved the house that stood by the water. There they seemed like a normal family. The huge oak tree that shaded the house, the dock they fished from, the times listening to opera on the radio with his father are all precious memories. Always a reader, he used a flashlight to read under the covers during the war.

While the foster family was good to him, there wasn't the love and nurturing a child would receive in a secure family setting with both parents. It was a strange upbringing that left Pat with issues that followed him into adulthood. Dean Meeks retired, and the Aldrichs took another live-in job with a wealthy family who owned automobile dealerships. In 1949, they worked for Broadway star Mary Martin. She lived in Greenwich, Connecticut, and was performing in *South Pacific* at the time. Pat was still living with the Jordans. His parents now lived further away so he saw them less frequently.

When Pat was sixteen he went to live with his parents. Carol had gone to school to be a beautician and worked in beauty salons in New Haven and Stamford, Connecticut. Vince was a waiter at the Union League Club in New Haven. Pat graduated from Hamden High School in 1954. His parents sent him to Suffield Academy in Suffield. Connecticut for one year. He liked the whole experience of going to a prep school. The only colored student in the school, he remembers that there were some students who couldn't accept that a Negro was attending a prep school. He excelled at football and baseball. Not so much at basketball. He was too short. His favorite was always football.

His father passed away from a heart attack on Labor Day 1955. Carol continued to work as a beautician until she moved to New York City in 1962. Pat was in the army at that time. After graduating from Suffield, he went to the University of Connecticut for one semester. Financial considerations sent him to West Virginia State College in Institute, West Virginia. The president of the college was a relative of sorts. His brother had been married to Carol's sister, Evelyn. Two of his first cousins were also at West Virginia State. He went to college for four years but didn't graduate. Pat was in the ROTC at college. He enjoyed the military life more than college life. In September 1961, he joined the Army. That's Pat's story. Despite his unusual upbringing, he flourished in the military. Those five promotions in five years are evidence of his success in overcoming the obstacles from his childhood.

One last thing. Pat wasn't the only nickname he had. Throughout his childhood, he was called Pokey because he did everything slowly. I don't know when he lost that nickname, but it's still appropriate. Pat thinks things through and doesn't move ahead until he's sure he's going in the right direction. Moving slowly is not a bad thing!

Here's a poem I wrote shortly after we became engaged in December 1966

PAT ALDRICH

You're not just Pat, or Sargeant Pat, or even Vince Collier Aldrich, Jr.
You're much more than just a name;
You're an individual composed of likes, dislikes, habits, mannerisms and
qualities of personality the make you, "you".
You're Tchaikovsky's 1812 Overture and Lorna Doone cookies.
You're a blue sweater thrown on a couch.
You're tight pants, football, smoke rings, and meatloaf.
You're gin and tonic and sown wild oats.
You're a man and a gentleman.
You're independent and tender.
You're indifferent and romantic.
You're impatient and deliberate
You're a half smile that rarely breaks through,
and eyes that speak from the heart.
You're Utrillo and lobster and popcorn and holding hands.
You're Canoe, Benson and Hedges, Rodin, Connecticut and David Chandler.
You "come out of a bag" and "go through a thing".
You're glasses that slip and mangy paws.
You're early American furniture and paisley ties.
A black Paris dress and beige lingerie,
Long natural loose hair, and a blue yarn kitten.
You can't stand knock knees, bell-bottom slacks,
thick ankles and airplanes.
You're cameras and darkrooms.
You're bowling and auto racing.
You're a Loden coat and a Class A Uniform.
You're "Hmmm" and "Jack!"
You're warmth and sensitivity.
You're the present and the future.
You're "you" and you're wonderful!

Poem, written by Sara, 1966.

CHAPTER TWENTY-SIX

THE CIVIL CEREMONY – BASEL, SWITZERLAND

June 1967 As we sped along the Autobahn toward Switzerland on June 12, 1967, the United States Supreme Court was handing down its Loving vs Virginia decision. That decision struck down all laws that prohibited mixed marriages. We were caught up in wedding plans. No time to bother with stateside happenings. It would be days before the news that mixed marriages were no longer illegal reached us. Two people in love, one white and one black, could now marry in all fifty states.

That perfect, sunny June day, Pat was at the wheel of my VW Beetle. With no speed limits on the Autobahn, we were flying. Wishing he was driving his Triumph Spitfire convertible, he managed to make the little green bug cruise between 70 and 80 mph. Our friends, Ollie and Dave, were with us to be witnesses at our civil ceremony the next day, so his two seater would have been a bit crowded. Even in my Beetle, they looked a little squished in the back seat. We had been witnesses at Dave and Ollie's civil ceremony in Germany two months earlier. Their coming to Switzerland with us was actually a honeymoon for them.

I could feel my muscles relaxing, my optimism returning and the tension headache fading. That headache had pestered me for weeks. There had been so many *what ifs*. "What if Pat's birth certificate hadn't arrived from the States in time? What if the Six Days War between Egypt and Israel hadn't ended yesterday? What if Pat hadn't been released from the hospital by now? His high blood pressure, brought on by stress, had been serious. I hadn't realized how much pressure he was under from his friends who opposed our marriage.

Closing my eyes, I decided that the late arrival of the birth certificate was really a blessing. The original wedding date was June 6, but we had changed it to the thirteenth because of the certificate.

So what if the wedding announcements had already been printed with the June 6 date. They weren't invitations. We didn't expect anyone but Pat's mother to come from the states for the wedding. Our friends in Germany didn't need printed invitations.

On the sixth, all military in Europe were on alert.

All leaves were canceled due to the Six Days War. My tension headache had reached its peak as we nervously waited to see if a June 13 wedding in Switzerland was going to happen. There's no way anyone can understand just how stressful it was as we followed the progress of the war. Now we were on our way to Basel. I was confident that tomorrow we would be married.

Looking back, I wondered how we ever got married at all! The amount of paperwork involved was unbelievable. Getting married in a foreign country was difficult. Being in the Army and getting married in a foreign country was twice as difficult. First, Pat had to get permission from his commanding officer to get married. That involved a marriage counseling session with the Legal Officer at 98th General Hospital and one with the Hospital Chaplain. Then there was a trip to the American Consulate in Frankfort, Germany, to get our marriage license. I wrote my father that "The American Consulate wouldn't accept Pat's birth certificate because it doesn't have the official seal of New York State. Pat has written home for another one, but it won't arrive in time for us to get married on the sixth . The Swiss authorities have to have the paperwork plus the birth certificates two weeks before the date we want to get married, so we have to put the wedding off until the thirteenth."

They say bad things come in threes. In our case it came in fours. The first was the birth certificate. The second was our dressmaker getting sick. By May 20th, she hadn't even gotten started on the dresses yet. We also found out that we weren't going to get the apartment we'd been negotiating for. The people who had it decided to stay. Then the announcements arrived with the wrong envelopes and had to be sent back. Thank goodness they weren't invitations! Despite all the potholes we encountered, we remained positive. In letters I wrote to my father before the wedding, I made no mention of the Six Days War between Israel and Egypt. That was probably the biggest roadblock to our June 13 civil ceremony in Basel. That war started on June 6th and my last letter was written on June 8th. I'm guessing I probably didn't want to worry him.

We began a search for another apartment. On June 2nd, I wrote my father that we had found an apartment. "It's rather old and run down, but it's only $57 a month. I think I'll be able to fix it up and make it homey and comfortable. We're moving all our things into the apartment tomorrow. We won't move in ourselves until we come back from Switzerland." I went to the big post exchange at the Wiesbaden Air Force Base to buy the household things we'd need in the apartment. If I hadn't, I wrote, "we'd be eating with our fingers off of paper plates, and I don't think that would be too good with Pat's mother visiting us." I spent every spare minute at the apartment, cleaning and getting it ready. It was really dirty. Ollie helped me in the mornings before I had to go to work at 1:00. We ran into some mice so I set a few traps and took care of them in short order. I have distinct memories of taking those mice out of the traps by their tails and throwing them out the second floor apartment window.

I still had trouble accepting the fact that in Europe, a church wedding was not legal unless there was a civil service first. That allowed the government to collect a tax for all ceremonies. In Germany, the tax for foreigners was one percent of their combined salaries. That was just a little steep for our pockets. We planned to honeymoon in Switzerland, so Pat wrote to the Zivilstandsamt in Basel to request information about marrying there. He received a letter back with all of the documents needed, the cost ($10.00), and the fact that foreigners were only married on Tuesdays. That was the reason for the original June 6 date and the later June 13 date. Each was a Tuesday.

We both had to request leave to have time off to get married. Such requests required exact dates. The original requests were for the fifth. At the last minute the requests had to be changed for the twelfth. We both held our breath until we received permission to go on "leave." Did any other couple have such difficulty with dates when trying to get married? How many couples didn't know if they were going to be able to get married because of a war? No wonder I had that tension headache!

Pat's birth certificate arrived in time. All the necessary

documents had been sent to Basel. Hotel reservations had been made. The War cooperated, and we arrived in Basel in the early afternoon on the twelfth. We checked in with the Zivilstandsamt Des Kantons Basel-Stadt to confirm our appointment in the morning. Things finally seemed to be going smoothly. I located a beauty salon close to the Hotel Kraft where we were staying and made an appointment to get my hair done late that afternoon. I intended to wear a copy of a Chanel suit we had made in Paris. It had cost an arm and a leg. Now, as I unpacked it, I realized I didn't like it! Given my light complexion the pale green tweed made me look washed out. Besides, who wore a wool suit in June? At least the jaunty green hat with a tiny veil matched the suit.

Coming out of the beauty saloon late that afternoon, my shoulders drooped, tears welled in my eyes and I was trembling. I looked horrible! My head was covered with tight curls. Some of them were already starting to unwind. I looked like Medusa! Ollie came to the rescue. I washed my hair, and she worked wonders with a simple style that looked fine. I couldn't do anything about the suit. At least I would only be wearing it for a short time. Bless his heart, the next morning Pat squeezed my hand and said, "You look beautiful." He looked pretty good himself in his new, tailored black suit.

The civil ceremony took place at what would be called a Courthouse in the United States. In Basel, it was the

Zivilstandsamt. The magistrate was a woman. One other couple was married at the same time. The ceremony was in English and very simple. We had to identify ourselves to the magistrate, say we wanted to be married and sign the required paperwork. The whole procedure lasted only a few minutes. With two copies of our marriage certificate in hand, we came out to find a warning notice on our car. We were parked in a no parking zone. At least it wasn't a ticket. That wouldn't have been a good way to start our married life.

Back at the hotel, we changed clothes and checked out. Before leaving for our honeymoon, we sat on the terrace overlooking the Rhine River and shared a celebratory non-alcoholic drink with Dave and Ollie. Sometime during our time in Basel, we managed to do a little sightseeing. We saw Rodin's statue, "The Burghers of Calais," and the cathedral. Pat took pictures. There were no pictures of the ceremony itself. No pictures allowed in the court house. It was just as well, as I wasn't happy with that expensive Paris suit. There was a picture taken on the terrace. Despite all the ups and downs, we were now officially man and wife. We were happy, relieved and ready for our two-day honeymoon in the Swiss Alps.

CANTON OF BASLE-CITY SWISS CONFEDERATION

Certificate of Marriage

Translated extract from the Register of Marriages Vol. 1967/1031
of the Registration District of Basle-City (Switzerland)

On this thirteenth day of June nineteen hundred and sixty-seven
marriage was contracted in BASLE between:

name: A l d r i c h , Vince Collier Jr.

marital status: single

nationality: citizen of the United States of America

residing in Washington (District of Columbia, USA), actually in Neubrücke/Nahe (Rheinland-Pfalz)

born at New York Brooklyn on March 17th, 1936

son of Aldrich, Vince Collier

and of his wife Carol, born Thurber

and

name: K u r t z , Sara Beth

marital status: single

nationality: citizen of the United States of America

residing in Oregon (Missouri, USA), actually in Neubrücke/Nahe

born at St. Joseph (Missouri) on June 5th, 1940

daughter of Kurtz, Willard Ivan

and of his wife Esther Elberta, born Kelly.

This is a true extract and translation from the Register of Marriages.

Basle, this 13th day of June 1967 ed

Registrar of Basle-City

CARLOTTA GSCHWIND

ZIVILSTANDSAMT

Sara and Pat's Marriage Certificate, 1967.

CHAPTER TWENTY-SEVEN

THE HONEYMOON

June 1967 Only two days for our honeymoon. We had planned those two days carefully. Dave and Ollie were taking their honeymoon right along with us. I wondered how many newlyweds took their witnesses on their honeymoon. Leaving Basel, we drove to Lucerne. Our reservations were at the Hotel Pilatus. We had stayed on Pilatus for the Fourth of July holiday in 1966. In a post card to my father dated from July 3, 1966 I wrote "What a fabulous view of the Alps!" When planning our honeymoon, the Hotel Pilatus immediately came to mind.

Perched on top of Mt. Pilatus, you reached the hotel via a cog railroad or a cable car. I'm not fond of heights, so both times we took the cog railroad. I learned later it was the steepest cog railroad in the world. Mt. Pilatus is seven thousand feet high. As the railroad climbed slowly to the top, the views of the valley, Lake Lucerne and the city of Lucerne were breathtaking. We passed through lush meadows filled with Alpine flowers. Later when I saw *The Sound of Music*, I wondered if those flowers were Edelweiss. I have distinct memories of dun colored cows with bells around their necks in all the meadows we passed. The sound of the bells was almost melodic. From the summit of Mt. Pilatus, you can see seventy peaks and five lakes. We were blessed with a beautiful, clear, sunny day.

There were two hotels on top of the mountain, but only one was in use. The original hotel was waiting to be renovated. The new hotel was circular and quite modern. At seven thousand feet, snow lingers most of the year. In June, there was lots and lots of snow. There were snow tunnels we walked through to get from one side of the hotel to the other. The views were spectacular. There is no way I can adequately describe how beautiful it was. To this day, almost fifty years later, I remember my awe at seeing those snow-covered Alps surrounding the hotel. Although new and modern, the hotel couldn't compete with the Alps. My memories are all about the mountains, the snow and the wonderful views.

I do know I wore a white, two piece pants suit and blended in with the snow. In a letter I received from Kelly just before we left for Switzerland, she said, "I just hope the sun is out over there and that you are not so excited as to not picture forever the beauty of it all. Happy Honeymooning."

The following letter was written to my father from Pilatus the day of our wedding, June 13, 1967.

"Dear Dad,

We were married at 10:00 this morning in Basel, and then we drove south to Lucerne and Mt. Pilatus to spend the night. We were here on the fourth of July weekend last year, and then we said what a beautiful place it would be to spend a honeymoon! There's about eight feet of snow on the ground, and they've dug tunnels through it so you can walk all around. The season doesn't open until mid-June so we are the only guests at the hotel. We are getting royal treatment: champagne, sirloin steak for dinner, fresh strawberries and cream, a beautiful room with bath, etc. We are also getting off-season rates: double room with bath, dinner and breakfast for two for $14. During the season, that would probably cost us about $20, maybe even more. Tomorrow we will head south and get further into the Alps. Oh yes, married life is great! Love, Sara Beth and Pat"

I wonder what that would cost today?

Mt. Pilatus was the perfect place to start our honeymoon. Early the next day, we took the cog railroad back down and were on our way to Grindelwald. We made stops in Interlaken and Brienz. All three villages are in the Bernese Oberland region of Switzerland and surrounded by mountains. Interlaken's name comes from the fact that it lies between Lake Thun and Lake Brienz. Brienz is known for its woodworking, which started in the early 1800's. As you drove down the main street of the village, every house or store had wonderful woodcarvings out front. Many of them were quite large and depicted animals such as bears, deer and dogs. We parked and strolled down the street, stopping in shops to admire the wonderful wood carvings. I bought a necklace of brown wooden beads that I treasured for many years. The beads were the only thing we could afford. I would have loved one of the intricate animal carvings. Even the smallest ones were beyond our pocketbook.

We walked down to the edge of Lake Brienz. It was a beautiful day and the lake was lovely. As we started to take pictures, we were approached by a police officer who told us picture taking was prohibited. It seemed a Swiss military base was using the lake for training their Air Force. Secret, sensitive stuff! Pat remembers seeing military planes flying low over the lake. Switzerland might be a neutral nation, but their military was prepared.

After lunch in Brienz, it was on to Grindelwald. Upon arrival, we found that there were no rooms available in the hotel itself. Instead, we got a charming little Swiss chalet on the grounds. The chalets were the equivalent of a standard hotel room. The huge bed covered with goose down comforters dominated the room. Although it was June, the elevation and snow made it chilly. Once the sun went down, it was downright cold. The comforters were much appreciated. Grindelwald was nestled under the towering Eiger, one of the highest peaks in the Alps. Behind the Eiger, the Jungfrau could be seen on a clear day. Unfortunately, there were clouds covering the mountain that day. The Jungfrau remained hidden.

Dropping off our luggage in the chalet, we took a walk down the main street. It was a lovely village, very Swiss. Even in 1967, Grindelwald was a tourist town. We discovered a miniature golf course. Our image of an authentic Swiss village was shaken but not destroyed by that discovery. We actually played a game of miniature golf with Dave and Ollie. It did seem strange to be playing mini golf in the middle of the Swiss Alps. It would have been more typical to go mountain climbing or attend a yodeling contest. We decided to have dinner at the hotel restaurant. Once again I don't remember the meal. A meal had to be very special like the Chateaubriand in Antwerp to get a place in my memory bank. The magnificence of the Alps dominated our stay in Grindelwald, as it had on Mt. Pilatus. One cannot get enough of the majestic views, the crisp, clean air and the whole ambiance of the little villages. Switzerland was the perfect place to honeymoon.

Checking out the next morning, we made our way back to

Germany. We returned on June 15, just three short days after leaving. So much had been crowded into those days. We were now officially married, but the church wedding was still to come. There was only one day until the church ceremony on the seventeenth with many last minute details to take care of including picking up Pat's mother. I'm still amazed that we were able to accomplish what we did during the five days from the thirteenth to the seventeenth.

CHAPTER TWENTY-EIGHT

THE CHURCH WEDDING

June 1967 Our second wedding was scheduled for Saturday, June 17, 1967, in the chapel at 98th General Hospital. We had reserved the chapel well in advance. Chaplain Vance Clark met with us for counseling. Our religious ceremony required a whole separate set of plans similar to plans made for any church wedding. I had designed the dresses for myself and Ollie, my maid of honor. Very simple. Made from what the Germans called half linen with Belgian lace sleeves. Pat's friend, Steve, made a drawing of the dress to show the local seamstress. Our dresses were alike except mine was white, and Ollie's was blue.

Wedding dress sketch, 1967.

Pat was in charge of getting the wedding bands. I didn't know it at the time, but he had ordered the bands at the same time as he had my engagement ring made back in December 1966. They were white gold to match my engagement ring.

We didn't have plans for special music at the wedding until Dr. Richard U. asked if he could sing. We were delighted to say yes. I described him in a letter to my father as "an operatic tenor who has sung professionally." He was to sing *Ich Liebe Dich* in German. The English translation is *I Love Thee*. Mrs. Michael D., wife of one of the hospital doctors, volunteered to play the piano. Our good friend, Joseph G., would walk me down the aisle and give me away. My one regret was that my sixty-nine year old father could not be there. Even at his age, he was helping his two brothers with one of the busiest times on the farm and couldn't get away. He was already planning to visit us in September just before the harvest season. He wrote, "I am sorry I can't be there now. But I just don't think I could have made it even if I wasn't helping on the farm." That was a reference to finances. A plane ticket to Europe was expensive.

We had the final fitting for our dresses. They were to be ready on the eighth . That day, I wrote my father, "We picked up our dresses today. They are just perfect. The material and cost of having them made came to about $25 apiece. That's a pretty inexpensive wedding dress."

Following our 2:00 ceremony in the chapel, there would be a reception at 7:00 p.m.. I sent out written invitations to the reception. It was to be held in the apartment of Sergeant and Mrs.

Clint A. They had volunteered to host , and we gratefully accepted. It was heartwarming that so many people were offering to help with the wedding. The German artist at the Service Club volunteered to inscribe the inside of our guest book. It read simply, " Mr. and Mrs. Vince Collier Aldrich, Jr., Neubrucke, Germany, 17 June 1967." The printing was beautiful.

Things were going smoothly when we discovered June 17 was a national German holiday. All shops would be closed. No flowers. No beauty saloons open to do our hair. Money works wonders, though. For a rather high fee, the hairdresser agreed to work on the morning of the seventeenth. The same applied to the florist who provided flowers. Adding the holiday closings to the problem list I wrote about back in Chapter Twenty-six brought the number up to five. Actually, it should be six because of the Six Day War between Israel and Egypt. That was definitely a problem. Thankfully our set of problems stopped at six. Not sure we could have handled any more!

Following the age-old tradition, I had something old, something new, something borrowed, something blue and a six pence in my shoe. The old was a tiny pearl pin that Pat's mother loaned me. It had been in her family for over one hundred years. I pinned it inside the bodice of my dress. The new was the dress. The borrowed was the veil. Ollie had worn it at her wedding. The blue was a garter. It was also borrowed from Ollie. She had brought me the six pence from their earlier trip to London.

Father's Day was June 11th that year. Somehow, I found the time to send Father's Day greetings and a small gift to my father. In his first letter addressed to SSG and Mrs. Vince C. Aldrich, he thanked me for his new passport holder. "I must get to work and get things together so I can make application for my passport. A holder is no good without something in it." September would arrive before we knew it.

We picked Pat's mother up at the Frankfort airport on June 16th. She was on a twenty-one day excursion planned especially for her. From Italy, she went to Paris. She flew from Paris to Frankfort and spent a week with us. Then it was on to London for four days before flying home. On the way home from the airport, we stopped for dinner at the Faust Haus in Bad Kreuznach. It was a very upscale restaurant that I knew from being stationed there. I was already aware that Pat's mother's tastes were on the expensive side.

To be honest, I was wary of meeting her for the first time. We couldn't have been more different. I was J.C. Penney. She was Saks Fifth Avenue. I was soda pop. She was a dry martini. What would she think of this Midwestern girl her son was marrying? We had a little time to get acquainted during the meal and drive home. I was able to relax when I sensed she was just happy that her son was finally getting married.

With the wedding the next day, there were a few last-minute

things to check, but everyone went to bed early to get a good night's sleep. Pat's mother was staying in the transient quarters on the base. There was no way she could stay with us. The new apartment was in disarray, with all our belongings still unpacked.

Up early Saturday morning, Ollie and I got our hair done. The wedding rehearsal went smoothly. Lt. Ben L. was there to take pictures. He was another volunteer who was greatly appreciated. Pat's good friend Steve had rotated back to the States in May, so he was not there to take pictures or take part in the wedding. We both missed him. Lt. L. took black and white photos during the rehearsal, before the ceremony, during the ceremony and at the reception. We have a 5" by 7" photo album of the best shots. Our guest book showed that thirty guests attended our wedding. To be honest, I wasn't aware of who was there and who wasn't. At the time, I was a nervous wreck. As Sergeant G. walked me down the aisle, I was trembling. His arm was gripped so tightly, it must have hurt. I looked toward the altar into the eyes of my smiling husband. This was the wedding that counted. My nerves calmed. My voice steadied. We looked at each other with love.

Two weddings in two countries in one week. A Six Day War. A combination of panic and elation. Highs and lows. Tears and laughter. I wrote my father that "Everything went beautifully at the church wedding. Pat's mother arrived on schedule, the flowers were delivered at the right time, the rehearsal went smoothly and the ceremony couldn't have gone better!" I didn't mention how nervous I was, or how happy we both were. Later in the same letter, I wrote, "We got a lot of nice gifts at our reception. Mostly, they were items that we wouldn't have purchased ourselves: silver serving dishes and trays, wine glasses, etc. We also got some useful everyday things like sheets and an iron. I'm going to be busy this next week writing thank you notes and addressing the announcements. I'll also try to write up a brief article for the Sentinel about the church wedding." Yes, the announcements with the correct envelopes had arrived.

I wore a little black dress at the reception, a direct contrast to the white pants suit I wore in Switzerland. Some might think wearing black on your wedding day would bring bad luck. Almost fifty years later we're still happily married. We not only survived that hectic time of two weddings all those years ago, we have thrived in the years since!

Sara and Pat, wedding, 1967.

Sara and Pat, reception, 1967.

CHAPTER TWENTY-NINE

THE AFTERMATH

Summer 1967 The wedding announcements went out shortly after the church wedding. Pat's mother said she was sending one hundred fifty. I don't think I even knew that many people that I felt needed to know I was married. A few more presents started to trickle in. His mother said most of the gifts from their side of the family would wait until we were back from Germany. She had given a list of things we needed to family and friends so they could pick what to give us. Shipping things to Germany didn't make sense when we would be back in the States in six months. My side of the family had sent money, which was greatly appreciated.

I asked my father in a letter if people knew about Pat? I wrote

"I would feel a little embarrassed to get gifts from people who didn't know because they might not have sent them if they did." I made sure all the aunts and uncles plus the closest cousins knew I was marrying a Negro. That information was included in letters I had written before the wedding. Dad's first cousin, Myrtle, and her husband sent a nice letter. Dad said in a letter that his brothers and sisters didn't seem excited and never said a word about my marriage to a colored man. We did receive letters from them. There was no indication that they were upset. Just wished us well. In a June 5th letter my father said, "I like to think we are at least halfway civilized. Jack married a girl from India. That's all I know." Jack was a nephew of one of my aunts. His wife was quite dark-skinned.

In the two and a half months between the church wedding and my father's arrival in Germany, a lot of events occurred. I passed out watching Pat play a softball game. Turned out I had low grade pneumonia. The antibiotics made me sicker than the pneumonia. I was also promoted to NGS 8, moving from my original NGS 6 status in less than two years. Ironically, shortly after the promotion, I turned in my resignation. It had to be received four months in advance. I had been transferred back to Neubrucke as Club Director just before the wedding.

We went on a Rhine River boat cruise. Got new furniture for our apartment from our landlord. At least it was new to us. Pat wrote my father that "After a month of marriage, I must say your daughter/my wife is an excellent cook. We don't have a chance to eat at home too much, but when we do it's great." That last surprised me, as our stove was a real antique. The oven definitely didn't heat evenly.

A letter from Kelly was received just before my father's September visit. She wrote, "Hope all three are well, and those wonderful plans for Willard are carried out without a hitch." When congratulating me on my promotion, she said "I want to say again and again you are tops with me." Kelly's letters always gave me a lift. She commented on the racial riots that were going on during that summer. "So the riots reached Pat's New Haven last night. Do you folks get our news re our summer disturbances. The riots play havoc in Atlantic Highlands, and a prowler was sent from the Park. It has changed my state of mind re my late nite walks from parties."

The Park was the trailer park where she lived. Atlantic Highlands was the town, so the disturbances as she called them, were close to home. I had to admit that Pat and I were too wrapped up in our own lives to pay much attention to the problems in the States. Pat's family never mentioned them, and my Midwestern relatives were not affected as were those who lived in the South or on either coast. Kelly ended her letter by saying, "Stop trying to push Pat and I together. We'll wind up hating each other!" I must have been singing Pat's praises a little too much. What she wrote was typical of her sense of humor.

During the months between the wedding and my father's arrival, all our letters were about his visit. I even sent him a travel book with the pages for the places we would be seeing marked. It had been decided that we would be spending two weeks in Italy. That was one of the places my father was most interested in seeing. He would be with us for a month. Never having traveled out of the country, he had questions about shots, electrical appliances, passports, what to pack and many other things.

CHAPTER THIRTY

DAD'S VISIT

September 1967 My father's full name was Willard Ivan Kurtz. The only people who ever called him Willie were Ada and Leland Warren. Nobody else could get away with that nickname. He was always Willard. He was born on July 14, 1898, so when he visited us in Germany, he was sixty-nine years old. Up to this point, I've referred to him as my father. I always used Dad in my letters to him. Once he became a grandfather he was known as Papa.

Dad served in World War I. He was a retired rural letter carrier. He had been a volunteer fireman. He was used to leadership roles in Kiwanis, the Masonic Lodge and the church. He bowled twice a week in the local league. He was an excellent carpenter and mechanic. In short, he was an accomplished man who contributed to his community. He helped with local elections. He chaired the Red Cross drive. He helped build cabinets for the senior center. He was well-liked and well-respected. I had always looked up to him. I recognized that I had a father to be proud of. He loved fishing and built two sixteen-foot fishing boats for use on local lakes. For over twenty-five years, he took fishing vacations in Minnesota with the Warrens. He was an excellent cook, a successful gardener, and a hard working farmer with his brothers.

On a more personal side, he didn't smile a lot but had a wry sense of humor. He only had a high school education, but his vocabulary was excellent. He was always there to help. You knew you could count on him. As a parent, he was firm but fair. There were rules that had to be followed. You knew you disobeyed those rules at your peril. A widower for seven years, he never thought to remarry. There was more than one older woman in Oregon who pursued him, and he would have been quite a catch. He belonged to the Oregon Seniors and frequently took bus trips with the group. He had never let me down. I hoped and prayed as he came to Germany to meet Pat that he wouldn't let me down in this the most important event in my life.

Dad had traveled pretty extensively in the United States. From California and Washington on the West Coast to New York and New Jersey on the East Coast, plus Wyoming, Colorado, Arizona and the Dakotas. That doesn't even count all the Midwestern states he spent time in throughout his life. Traveling to Europe was just a little more challenging, as I discovered when I began work for the Army. Language, money, customs and food were all different. In the letters we exchanged between June and his arrival on September 1, he had many questions. We had decided on a self-drive trip to Italy. Italy won out over France and Spain, probably because of all the Christian history connected with Rome and the vast treasure of artistic work to be found. I sent him a brochure on the tour we planned to take, advising him to do some advance reading. From experience, I knew you enjoyed a trip much more if you had a knowledge of and an appreciation for the incredible places you would be seeing.

I advised him on what clothes to bring. There was a detailed list of everything from a light weight suit to a jacket for chilly evenings. Italy would be warmer than Germany, but he would be spending equal time in both countries. As September got closer, we had some cold days in Germany. I told him to bring some long johns. When he asked about money, I recommended travelers checks in twenty dollar increments.

As we would be using my VW Beetle for the trip to Italy, I suggested he bring two small suitcases instead of one large one. Not much trunk space in a bug. He was using a travel agent. I'm sure they confirmed all his reservations for him. He did have some problems getting his passport because he didn't have a birth certificate. On August 5th I wrote, "I'm rather worried about your passport difficulties. I don't know what we'll do if you can't come over on September 1st". Fortunately it arrived on August 23rd. Usually it takes four or five weeks to get a new passport. Dad's arrived in two weeks .

Dad was one hundred percent German. He was looking forward to seeing the country of his ancestors. I wrote out a tentative itinerary that included time in Bavaria and the Black Forest. We were scheduled to leave on September 5 and not arriving in Italy until late on the eighth. That allowed time to visit such places as Oberamergau and King Ludwig's Fairy Tale Castle as we passed through southern Germany.

Unfortunately, those plans fell through when I needed to change my name on my driver's license. That wasn't as easy as it was in the States. In order to cut through the Army's red tape, we had to go to the Army headquarters in Heidelberg. By the time I got my new driver's license, several days had been wasted. We had to cut out the time we had meant to spend on the way to Italy and just drive straight there.

Dad arrived on schedule at 8:50 on the morning of September 1. We picked him up at the Frankfort Airport. He was tired but doing well for a man his age with jet lag. I was just happy to see him after two years and thought he looked wonderful. Being the staid German he was, he just shook Pat's hand and said it was good to finally meet him. I think he was a little surprised at the primitive conditions we were living in. Any house over a one hundred years old in a small German town was not going to have modern conveniences. He didn't say anything, but I'm sure he would have preferred a shower instead of the old-fashioned bathtub where we had to heat the water using briquettes in a little stove attached to the tub. He amazed Pat by carrying a large load of those briquettes from the cellar all the way up to our second floor apartment without breaking a sweat. Dad was in great shape. He never even complained about the lumpy mattress on his bed in our guest room. My back would have been protesting.

Dad got to see the Service Club where I worked. He spent the first day with me there after he arrived. We took him to visit as many of the local sights as we could during those first few days. Pat and I were both working, but I had mornings free to show Dad around. We did allow him a day to recover from his trip. Again, it was amazing how quickly he rebounded. He actually did better than I did when I first arrived, and he was forty-two years older. Guess all that farm work kept him fit.

I have no letters to refresh my memory of what we did during Dad's visit. No need to write each other when he was right there with us. Pat remembers things I don't. I remember things that he has no recollection of. Hopefully between the two of us, our account of Dad's twenty-eight days in Europe is fairly accurate.

Our drive-it-yourself tour allowed us more freedom, as we weren't connected with a group. The seventy-five dollars per person took care of our hotels, all our meals, and the taxes, service charges (tips) and guide fees for the whole time we were in Italy. It was a very reasonable way to travel. We followed an itinerary provided by the tour company, just making sure we arrived at our hotels by a certain time. We had lots of freedom in what we saw and did each day. The only out-of-pocket expenses would be the gas for the car and the souvenirs we bought. Gas was very expensive in Europe, but because we were military, we bought gas coupons from the Army that allowed us to get gas at about half-price. Twenty-five gallons of gas cost about $6.35. That is just a little over twenty-five cents a gallon. Compare those prices to what a similar trip would cost today!

The drive-it-yourself tour was only for Italy. Getting there and returning to Germany, we were on our own. During those times, we traveled through Germany, Austria, Switzerland and France. All told, my father was able to visit five countries during his stay. My little VW Beetle performed admirably, covering almost three thousand miles on that trip. The only problem we encountered was in the Alps when we were hit from the rear as we drove through the Brenner Pass between Austria and Italy. The back of our car was dented in so the door to the engine couldn't be opened.

Remember, the engine was in the rear. We needed access to the engine to check the oil and other fluids. Once again, we were lucky, as the man who hit us had a heavy rope in his trunk. He attached it to the fender of our car and the front of his car. With a couple of tugs, the dent moved enough so we could have access to the engine. We exchanged sorrys and thank yous and continued on our way. Most of our conversation had been conducted in gestures, shrugs and facial expressions, as none of us spoke Italian, and the gentleman didn't speak English.

As we drove through the Alps, there was a sign indicating that Hannibal with his elephants crossed the Alps at that point. Because of his love of history, Pat was more impressed by that than Dad or I were. It was certainly a remarkable feat. I couldn't imagine elephants climbing those mountains.

Our first night in Italy was spent in the town of Verona. We didn't see much, as we arrived late and left early the next morning. I distinctly remember being thrilled that I was in the town where Romeo and Juliet's tragedy was played out. I had always loved Shakespeare. On to Venice where we took a gondola ride, rode a vaporeto down the Grand Canal to the Lido on the Adriatic Sea, watched a glass blowing demonstration, marveled at St. Marks Cathedral and sat in St. Mark's Square while enjoying lunch. The story behind the Bridge of Sighs was told by our guide, along with other tales about the Doges (dukes), Venice ruling the seas and the fact that it is slowly sinking into the ocean. Being in the city of Shakespeare's *Merchant of Venice* had me remembering the pound of flesh from the play. A fond memory is of the hundreds of pigeons in St. Marks Square rising like a cloud when the bell tower rang the hour.

Our next destination was Florence. Before entering the city, we stopped atop a hill where a copy of Michelangelo's *David* looked out over Florence. The view was breathtaking. The Duomo (Santa Maria del Fiore) and the Palazzo Vecchio (town hall) dominated the city's skyline. The red rooftops spread out before us, and the Arno River made its winding way through the city. Cradle of the Renaissance, home of the Medicis, depository of many of the world greatest works of art, Florence was a feast for our senses. We saw the original *David* in the Galleria dell Academia, gazed at Botticelli's *Venus* in the Uffizi Gallery, and were dwarfed by the Neptune Fountain in the Palazzo della Signoria. We spent time in the magnificent Gallery of Statues adjacent to the Signoria.

The Ponti Vecchio that spanned the Arno River was the only bridge left standing after World War II. The many shops along the edge of the bridge were supported by stilts. I managed to get across the bridge without buying anything. Most dramatic were the doors of the cathedral (Duomo) that showed the stains of the water level from the massive flooding of the previous year. We saw them as sections of *The Gates of Hell* were being restored. Once again my love of Shakespeare came into play as much of *All's Well that Ends Well* is set in Florence. I felt the presence of his characters as we walked through the city.

Not being a demonstrative person, it was hard to tell Dad's reaction to all that we were seeing. Neither Pat nor I have any memories of his expressing his feelings about any of the works of art or impressive buildings. He was a man of few words, but I like to think I would have immediately known if he was bored or displeased. In a way, his not saying anything meant he was content and enjoying himself. Rome was the city he had expressed a desire to see. I anticipated his reactions there might be more evident. Who cannot be awed by the Sistine Chapel?

Rome was our next stop, and we spent the most time there. The weather was not cooperative, as it rained a good part of the time. Traffic was horrible. You took your life in your hands when you entered a traffic circle. The Romans drove like maniacs. As soon as we reached our hotel, we parked the car and didn't move it until we were ready to leave. Taxis were plentiful and inexpensive. We also used buses to get around the city. I remember getting in a taxi and just saying the single word *Moses.* The driver took us directly to the church San Peitro in Vincoli where Michelangelo's statue was housed.

The five most visited sights in Rome were the Colosseum, the Trevi Fountain, the Pantheon, the Roman Forum and St. Peters

Cathedral. We saw all five plus much more. We threw coins in the Trevi Fountain to bring us good luck. It was also to ensure that we would return to Rome. The good luck part has worked as we've had a wonderful almost fifty years of marriage. The return to Rome doesn't look too promising. Age, health and finances appear to be standing in the way.

We climbed the 138 Spanish Steps, strolled down the leading shopping street Via del Condotti, visited St. Paul Outside the Walls church with the portraits of each pope in frieze around the upper walls and spent time at the grandiose Monument of Vittorio Emanuele II, who unified Italy. We saw the beautiful *Pieta* in St. Peters and gazed in awe at Michelangelo's Sistine Chapel ceiling. Even Dad was impressed. Our guided tour was mostly through the ancient Roman ruins, including the Colosseum. My father was moved when we saw the tiny cell where the imprisoned St. Paul wrote his epistles to the churches. It was one of the few times he expressed his emotions. My Shakespeare self appreciated the setting for *Julius Caesar*. I could almost hear Caesar saying "et tu Brute?"

It was hard to leave Rome, as it meant our time in Italy was almost over. We had one last major stop to see the Leaning Tower of Pisa. That's the only note-worthy thing to see in that city. When we were there the tower was surrounded by scaffolding as efforts were made to keep it from completely tumbling.

We traveled along the Mediterranean Sea as we drove north toward France. Pat feasted on mussels when we stopped at a little village for lunch. He loved all kinds of seafood. I remained allergic to shellfish. We said goodbye to Italy as we entered the Monte Blanc Tunnel that would take us to France. Completed in 1965, the tunnel, at 7.2 miles, was the longest in the world. Pat being slightly claustrophobic was not comfortable during the drive. We ended up in Chamonix, France, but didn't stop. Geneva, Switzerland, was our destination that day.

Tired and knowing we had a long drive ahead of us the next day, we only spent the night in Geneva. The one thing we saw the next morning was the Palace of Nations situated on the north side of Lake Geneva. Pat remembers seeing a very rare Lamborghini Miera flying down a street in Geneva. According to him, Dad's reaction was priceless. He had never seen such a car. The high-pitched roar of the engine startled him. He stared and asked, "What was that?"

We arrived back in Neubrucke that night. It had been a wonderful two weeks. Pat and I had to work the next day, but Dad was able to relax and recuperate. During the next week, we took him to see some of our favorite places in the area that we had missed the first week. Lichtenburg Castle, Idar Oberstein and Trier were close enough to enjoy in a few hours. Dad also spent time with me in the Service Club. He seemed to enjoy talking to the young men who came to the club every day, and they enjoyed listening to him. I was surprised how he opened up to them and told stories even I didn't know. Perhaps Dad reminded them of their own grandfathers back home. One night we took him to the NCO Club to hear the El Jades band. I'm not sure how he liked that. The place was jam-packed and the music loud. We didn't stay long!

We took Dad to the airport in Frankfort on September 29th. In my first letter to him after he got home, I wrote, "By now you should be back in the groove and, I hope, rested up. I imagine everyone in church today wanted to know all about the trip. I wish we could have shown you more, but things did get pretty hectic around here after we got back from Italy. At least you got to see five different countries. How did everyone like their gifts?" At the end of my next letter, I wrote, "I'm glad you enjoyed your trip to Europe. It was so good to see you again. We hope you feel more at ease now, and you can tell Alice and Kenneth, the Warrens, Myrtle and Bill, etc. about Pat. Even though you never said one way or the other, I hope you like him. I know he likes you."

I was so relieved that Dad finally got to meet Pat in person. In his reserved manner, he would never have been effusive in any of his reactions or responses. It was enough that he seemed content and not as worried about us. I'm sure with the racial situation in the States at the time, he still had concerns for our safety once we returned home. Any concerns he had about Pat's character, intelligence and abilities, had I hope been laid to rest.

CHAPTER THIRTY-ONE

RETURN TO THE STATES

January 1968 As Christmas approached in 1967, Pat and I were making plans to return to the States in January. I had resigned from my position as Club Director at Neubrucke Service Club. Pat was on a Christmas schedule, working one day on and one day off. My last paycheck was to have arrived on December 18th when everyone else got paid. That didn't happen. We had counted on that paycheck to handle last-minute expenses, including the shipping of my VW Beetle back to the States on December 20th . The check didn't arrive until the end of the month, and we had to cash bonds to ship the car. It was picked up on schedule by the shipping company and was on its way to the States. Once the check arrived, we were finally able to close our bank accounts and transfer money to my account in Missouri.

I had handwritten forty-five notes in our Christmas cards informing everyone that we were returning to the States and giving them our temporary address with Pat's aunt in Brooklyn, NY. We purchased a ten-thousand-dollar life insurance policy for Pat to replace the one he would lose when he got out of the Army. Pat was working in the photo lab every spare minute to print all the pictures from our travels. Who knew when he would get access to a dark room once we were home?

It was our last Christmas in Germany, but our first as a married couple. We received many presents from my Dad and Pat's mother. All things we could use. After Christmas, I wrote Dad about our Christmas Eve: "At 7:00 there was a Christmas Cantata in the chapel that was really beautiful. At 9:30 we went to the NCO Club dancing." Despite Pat not being a good dancer, he managed to shuffle through the slow dances and did a little better with the fast ones. We danced one last time to what we considered our song, *Strangers in the Night* by Frank Sinatra. We got home at 12:30 and decided to open our presents, since I would be busy cooking the next day. We invited three guys from Pat's office to Christmas dinner. I had never cooked a turkey before. Our oven is much hotter in back, so we had to keep turning the turkey so it would cook evenly. It didn't turn out too badly.

There was actually a mail call at the hospital on Christmas Eve which was a Sunday. We received ten cards that day, plus a letter from my father. We didn't hear anything from Robert and his wife. I had sent them a Christmas card saying we hoped to be able to stop and see them when we drove to Missouri in February. That must have panicked them. We hadn't heard from them since the previous Christmas, when we announced our engagement. It wasn't until January 1968 that we finally got a letter from them. In addition to saying he thought we had made a mistake and he didn't want to be any part of that mistake, Robert said that he felt our staying in Oregon for nine or ten days would bring unpleasantness to our father. In a letter to Dad I wrote, "I want you to give me an honest answer. Will our staying in Oregon bring any unpleasantness to you? If so, we will stay only long enough to get my things and say hello to the family, probably two or three days. You mentioned in a letter shortly after you got home that the word was out, but you never said anymore. Do a lot of people in town know? If so, what has their reaction been?"

My father replied immediately, saying we were welcome to stay as long as we liked. He also enclosed a letter my cousins, Helen and Carl, had written to him on December 26th. "I just wouldn't hurt you for the world if I could avoid it, but for all concerned, Carl and I think it would be better if we didn't see them. We know we couldn't be natural, like this was any ordinary marriage. It's possible we would cause more hurt by our prejudicial attitude than by avoiding the situation altogether. I do hope you understand and won't let this come between our friendship. We are not alone in feeling this way, and I'm sure Sara Beth is going to have to realize many people will never approve of what she has done. I only hope their feelings for one another are strong enough to be happy with such odds against them. I hope I haven't let you down too much, but had to let you know."

My father wrote them saying he was sorry, and if there was a change in their thinking they could always come up. In his letter to me he said, *"I wouldn't feel too badly about this. Now on the other hand, I talked to Myrtle G. on the phone when I was in St. Joe a while back, and I am to call her when you get here. She wants us and Pearl to come down for a meal. I think this more than compensates.*

"The above has caused me to come to the conclusion that you cannot go calling on people unless you are invited. I do not know myself how widely this is known. I have not been approached by anyone. At church on the seventh, I was talking to Elizabeth E. and Violet and Harry. Elizabeth asked if you would be here any time, that she did want to give you a little gift. So I just up and asked them if they had heard anything about Pat. Harry said, 'Who is Pat?' I said, 'My son-in-law.' They all said no, so I told them of Pat's ancestry.

You will never guess what Harry said!! 'Let me just ask you one question, are they happy?' I said, 'Yes, I am sure of that.' 'Well, he said, 'that is all that matters.' Elizabeth and Violet were of the same opinion. There was no hesitation on the part of any of them in stating that the sooner we accept these things, the better off we will be. Then I told Rev. S. and Mrs. S. at church one day. They wanted to know when you would be here because they wanted to meet you both. I think I told you that I had told Lloyd and Alice, Mrs. G. and Mrs. H. and Eldora." So far, only my cousins in St. Joe had a problem with our marriage. We definitely wouldn't be stopping to see them.

Regarding my brother's letter, my father wrote, "They called and said they had a card from you saying something about seeing them. I just laughed at them. I asked if he had ever written and expressed himself, and he said no. I had asked him twice to do this. I told him, 'Sara Beth knows how you feel, but you better write and tell her or you will have visitors! No kidding, I sure laughed at him whether he liked it or not. That was over two weeks ago, and I have not heard from them."

He then went on to write about his own reactions. It was the first time he had really opened up about his struggle to accept our engagement back at the beginning of 1967. *"Now about me, I have to admit that after your announcement last December, I had a rough time trying to think this out. My first concern was for you, and then I began to realize that there was maybe as much concern for myself. After I realized this and got myself out of the picture, then things began to shape up and the picture was not nearly so disconcerting. I want to assure you that if I had not got this worked out in my own mind, I would not have come to Europe to visit you. I think I owed it to Pat to get acquainted with him on neutral ground. I am very thankful and happy that I was privileged to do this."*

That letter from my father is one that I treasure. My father was a very wise man. Reading it forty-nine years later, I had tears in my eyes. It brought home just how my father and most of my family and friends accepted us. Those who didn't were by far in the minority.

Back in Germany, we continued our preparations for returning to the States. The Army packers came on Friday, December 29, to box everything up to be shipped home. They knew their job, and it only took them one-and-a-half hours to pack everything. We worked like little beavers to be ready for them Friday at 8:00 a.m. In my January 1, 1968 letter, I wrote, "When they were done, we had twenty-two separate containers totaling about nine hundred lbs. We were authorized five thousands lbs. So we barely scratched the surface. The packers said with five thousand lbs., we could have shipped three complete rooms of furniture." Once they took everything away, we moved into the transient quarters on the base.

We rang in the New Year at the NCO Club. We reserved a table with another couple. The cost was five dollars per couple and that included a free bottle of champagne and breakfast at 3:00 in the morning. Of course, there were also free hats, noise makers, confetti and streamers. There were two bands: One played til 2:00 a.m., and the second took over and played until the Club closed at 5:30 a.m. We left about quarter to four, but a lot of people stayed until the very end. The breakfast was really good. They served scrambled eggs, ham, fried potatoes and toast. That was a lot for $5.00. Things were certainly less expensive forty-nine years ago. It was our first New Years as a married couple. We celebrated heartily. There was about four inches of snow on the ground when we walked the two blocks to our quarters. We were glad we didn't have to drive.

Pat was to drive his car to the shipping company on January 7, but we woke up to eight inches of snow and an order from Army Headquarters in Heidelberg that no vehicles were to leave any military post until further notice. I wrote, to my father, "The MPs were stationed at the gate to keep any cars from leaving. Well, that rather put a stop to Pat's driving the car to Frankfurt, but he still had to get there that night so he would catch his plane the next day."

Pat got his commanding officer to authorize a power of attorney for me so I could take care of the car after he left. It wasn't really as simple as that, though. Pat took the train to Frankfurt and left for the States on Monday. I was leaving on Wednesday so there were only two days to get the car shipped. That little Spitfire was completely covered under a foot of snow. It took four sturdy GIs from the Service Club to dig it out. I was holding my breath, hoping it would start after all the wet and cold. It purred like a kitten.

The shipping company picked it up on Tuesday. We had canceled Pat's liability insurance as of January 9 when the marine insurance took over. It was a close call. In Dad's letter I wrote, “Believe me, this has been one hectic day! I think my blood pressure is way up there. I just hope we don't have all these complications when I get ready to leave on Wednesday. Keep your fingers crossed for us.”

By the time I arrived in the States, Pat was officially discharged from the Army and staying with his aunt in Brooklyn. He met my plane at McGuire Air Force Base in New Jersey, and we took a bus to Port Authority in New York. From there, a taxi got us to Brooklyn. Remember our cars where somewhere out on the Atlantic. Exhaustion was setting in, and I dozed in the taxi. It wasn't until later that I realized I had left my Olympus Pen F camera in the taxi. We called the taxi company. Of course, it was long gone. Someone got a great camera. It was a half frame camera, so a roll of 24 film got you 48 pictures. I don't remember everything that was on the camera, but there were Christmas and snow pictures.

One of the first things we did on arrival was call Dad and Kelly to to let them know we were back safely. In her January 11 letter, Kelly wrote, "Oh, thank you for the phone call! I can hardly believe I've talked with you. Vince, I will never be more surprised or pleased than when the pictures arrived. You must like your old Auntie to take that trouble. Thank you dear. Thank you. And the beautiful, exquisite gold pin. Don't you folks spoil me! There is so much to talk about. I hope you won't be in a hurry when you come down, 'cause I'll be just dumb at first, my mind a complete blank. Here's a New Year wish for every good thing to come your way. Good jobs, good apt. etc." Dad wrote, also on January 11, "It was real nice to talk to both of you Friday night and to know that you made connections. Now if your cars and personal property get here, you can begin to formulate plans."

That was exactly what we had to do during the next few weeks. We were home safely, but a whole new life awaited us in the States.

CHAPTER THIRTY-TWO

OUR NEW LIFE

January 1968 Big city life was vastly different from our life in the military. Pat had lived in Harlem at one point and had family in Manhattan and Brooklyn. I had never lived in a city. Most of my family was over a thousand miles away. Kelly was the closest in New Jersey. Adjusting to city life was not going to be easy for me. Keeping busy with finding housing, jobs and learning to use the subway would hopefully keep me from stressing about all the other unknowns.

Our first priority was finding a place to live. We couldn't impose on Pat's Aunt Mary forever. Here, we had help from our friends, Dave and Ollie. They had returned to the States shortly after they were in our weddings. They spent three months trying to find a furnished apartment. They had warned us they were "as scarce as hen's teeth." They finally gave up and took an apartment in a new complex called Lefrak City in Queens. Their experience told us not to waste time trying to find a furnished apartment. After seeing Dave and Ollie's apartment, we went directly to Lefrak City and signed a lease for a one bedroom apartment. We would move in March 1st. Pat's family managed to provide us with the basics in furniture; three-quarter bed, a dinette set, a chest of drawers, a vanity and a coffee table.

Lefrak City had just about everything you could want within easy walking distance. Supermarkets, department stores, movie theaters, banks. Dave and Ollie paid $160 a month. That was quite reasonable for New York City. With housing taken care of, we turned to finding jobs. I had an appointment with the State Employment Agency. Amazingly, I received several possible job offerings. I interviewed at The Wartburg Lutheran Home for the Aging in Brooklyn for a position as Activity Director. Working with the elderly would certainly be different from the young GIs in the Army. At least I would be in my field of recreation. When I was offered the job starting in March, I didn't hesitate to accept.

Pat returned temporarily to the Post Office, where he had worked before going into the Army. Dave once again helped out. He was working for a company called Victor Comptometer Corp.

They dealt with the new emerging computer industry. Back in 1968, computers were as big as a room. The laptop and even the desktop were far in the future. Dave helped Pat get a job at Victor. The two friends got in on the ground level in computer programming and systems analysis. Pat was to work in the computer field for thirty years. I worked as a recreation therapist in health care facilities for more than thirty-eight years. We had found our niche.

With jobs and housing taken care of, we began to plan a trip to Missouri to visit my family. We planned to drive across country in my little Beetle and hoped to leave around February 1st. Writing to Dad, I said, "My car finally arrived in port today, and we hope to be able to pick it up tomorrow afternoon. I'm going to take my driver's test tomorrow morning early." Since I had a valid Missouri driver's license, I only had to take the written test. No problem passing it. Pat's Army license wasn't recognized. He had to take both the written and the driving test. By the time he got his interim license, and his Triumph arrived, it was well into February. Not much time left for our Missouri trip.

As soon as I got my driver's license, we went to New Jersey to see Kelly. I was anxious for her to meet Pat. I had no idea she had expressed doubts about our marriage in her letters to Dad. Her letters to us were welcoming. I was sure she would love Pat. We went on a Friday and only stayed a short time. Didn't want to get into weekend/rush hour traffic. As I was doing all the driving and not used to city driving, I was nervous. Kelly was one to express her emotions. She was effusive in her welcome and talked almost non-stop throughout the visit. Lots of questions and observations. In her note after our visit, she wrote, "Oh Thank You, Thank You darlings for coming down Friday. . . Best to your Mother and Aunt, Pat. Love to you Guys and Good Luck." That was Kelly. Everything capitalized.

We had also gotten a letter from the Warrens welcoming us home. Dad had visited the Warrens with pictures of his time in Europe. Uncle Leland wrote, "We had a great visit with Willard. He brought his pictures. . .Ada joins me in welcoming you back to the States and assuring you that we want to see you both when you are out this way. Your old, aging, decrepit, and still battling, Uncle Leland."

When we did get to Nebraska to see them, Uncle Leland intended to ask the church session if there would be a problem with us staying in the Manse (the house owned by the church where the minister lived) . Not only was permission given, but three different church families offered to house us when we arrived. We stayed in the Manse. Every trip to Missouri, we tried to visit them. They were always an inspiration to both of us. We missed them terribly when they both passed.

On one trip to Nebraska to see the Warrens. we made a stop in

Glen Wood, Iowa, to visit their daughter and her family. As we reached the city limits, there was a big billboard announcing that Glen Wood was the home of the John Birch Society. We almost turned around and left. The John Birch Society had opposed the Civil Rights movement, saying it was backed by Communists. Knowing the town housed members of that Society filled us with trepidation. We decided to go ahead with our visit. There were no problems, but we didn't stay long!

Our trip to Missouri went smoothly. There were no issues of any kind. As I said earlier, the people in my home town seemed to be colorblind. Of course, those that had a problem with our marriage had already made their feelings known. It was their problem, not ours. We had a wonderful visit with my aunts, uncles and many Kurtz cousins. After we returned to New York, Dad wrote, "I want to tell you how much I enjoyed having both of you here even though it was for such a short time. Violet M. called this morning, and she is mailing you a wedding present (they were gone while we were there, so she couldn't deliver it in person). She said she had talked to Nina F. and she had commented that she was impressed and found Pat an interesting and superior person." I always felt that once people met Pat, they would understand why I married him.

Shortly after we arrived back in the States, Dad had written, "Well, I am sure this is an exciting time for both of you. Your service time is behind you, and now you will seek to establish yourselves in your niche in a great big world. It should be a real challenging time from here on." Now, almost fifty years later, I can safely say we met that challenge and established ourselves quite successfully in the lives we chose. After living seven years in Queens, we moved to upstate New York and bought a house in the little town of Florida, New York. Our son, Jason, was born in 1971 when we lived in Queens. Stacie was born in 1977 in Goshen, New York. Dad and Pat's mother each visited us twice a year. We managed to get to Missouri once a year. Pat's mother lived in Manhattan part of that time but then moved to Washington, DC, when she retired so she could be close to her sisters.

We created a new life once back in the States. Things moved along through the years as we raised our family and progressed in our careers. While I had lost some of my family, those who accepted us more than made up for that loss. The concerns of our loved ones that we would experience hatred and prejudice from the society in which we lived and worked didn't happen on any large scale. We frequently got stares and glares from strangers, but no burning of crosses or physical attacks. In the workplace, we experienced no discrimination. Our philosophy continued to be that we didn't have a problem. It was those who disapproved of us who did.

CHAPTER THIRTY-THREE

THE BICENTENNIAL YEAR

July 1976 Nineteen hundred seventy-six, the country's Bicentennial year, but to me it was the year I got my brother back. Robert broke off all contact with me in 1967 because of my marriage to a Negro. During the nine years of our estrangement, my father kept us abreast of each others activities. Our life went on without Robert. We bought a home, moved to upstate New York and had a son. In 1976, I was pregnant with our second child.

The entire nation was gearing up for a big celebration on the Fourth of July. Millions of cities and towns, large and small, were planning events to honor our nation's 200th birthday. All across the country, bands were practicing lively marches. Choruses were rehearsing for musical extravaganzas. In small towns, everyone got involved. My hometown, Oregon, Missouri, was making big plans. Red, white, and blue bunting would drape the whole town. The 100-year-old bandstand in the courthouse square got a fresh coat of paint. The concert on the bandstand would feature Sousa marches. Men were growing beards, and women were sewing period costumes. There would be Martha Washington, Betsy Ross, Indian Chiefs, Union and Confederate soldiers, and even Benjamin Franklin to be seen in town during the celebration. Every organization, church and business had volunteers working to finish the floats for the parade. A lot of crepe paper found its way onto those floats. In rural Midwest towns, the parades would feature handmade floats, dog carts, tractors, bicycles and horses. Big city parades would have professionally made floats, politicians, military units, and huge bands with two to three hundred members. The Oregon High School Band had sixty.

The Presbyterian minister, who was tall and had a striking resemblance to Abraham Lincoln, would portray Lincoln from the pulpit that Sunday. His rendition of *The Gettysburg Address* would open the service. Horse drawn-wagons filled with hay would provide rides around the square. Demonstrations of apple cider making and horseshoeing were planned. A huge fire pit would roast a whole pig. The corn on the cob, homemade apple sauce and roast pig dinner would go for $2.00. Or you could choose a fried fish dinner from the Kiwanis stand, also $2.00.

Long before the Fourth of July, Pat and I made plans to celebrate the Bicentennial in my hometown. My relatives and friends had welcomed us when we made our first visit to Oregon after returning to the States from Germany in 1968. Through the years, I always looked forward to my visits home. Plans were to fly into Kansas City a few days before the Fourth. Those plans were scrapped when I learned I was pregnant. The doctor said no flying in the first trimester. We made arrangements to drive, taking two and a half days to make a trip that takes two hours by plane. There were strict instructions to stop every hour so I could walk and stretch. Those restrictions were deemed necessary because of my mother's history of nine miscarriages. Things got more complicated when Dad called to say he would be going to Athens, Ohio, at the end of June for my brother's graduation from the University of Ohio with his Doctorate in Education. We had to schedule our arrival in Oregon to coincide with Dad's return from Ohio.

One evening a week before we were to leave for Missouri, my husband answered the phone, turned to me and said, “It's your brother.” I wasn't sure I had heard right and said, “Who?” “Your brother,” he repeated. I still couldn't quite comprehend and said, “Robert?” As if I had more than one brother. “Yes” was Pat's response. As I took the phone, I shook my head as if trying to clear nine years of cobwebs. My knees felt wobbly, and I had to sit down. After all those years of silence, Robert had called to invite us to his graduation.

It was a short conversation, just the basic information about the time and place of the graduation ceremony. When we talked on the phone that night, it was as if those nine years of silence had disappeared. He did not, and I dared not, mention anything that had happened during those years. I certainly wasn't going to ask him on the phone why he had changed his mind. Questioning and confrontation would do nothing to heal the breach that had existed for so long.

Not only were we invited to the graduation, we were also invited to stop at Robert's home in Shaker Heights, Ohio, on our way back from Missouri. There, we would have more time to get reacquainted and hopefully put the past completely behind us. We talked again before leaving. That conversation was also short and to the point, just giving directions and arranging to meet after the ceremony. I had reservations about that meeting, not sure what to say and what not to say. Did I want to probe and find out why the apparent change of heart after all these years? Do I just ignore the silence of almost a decade? I finally decided to follow my brother's lead. I suspected he would have planned what he was going to say, and there was no way I could know where that would lead. After all, he was the one who had rejected us.

The time arrived to begin our journey across country. We lived in New York and had almost fifteen hundred miles to cover. The stop in Ohio would add another day to our trip West. Traveling with our five-year-old son, Jason, turned out to be a challenge. It was a good thing the doctor had ordered hourly stops for me, since five-year-olds need bathroom breaks and time to run around.

Arriving on the University of Ohio campus the day of the big event, we promptly got lost despite my brother's directions. As on most older campuses, there were many brick buildings that looked alike. When we finally did locate the auditorium, there was no time to find my brother's wife, Carol, or my father. The proceedings were about to start, and we took what seats were available with seconds to spare. I remember feeling nervous and out of breath. Our seats were high up in the auditorium. Our rush to park, get into the building, and climb all the stairs had taken their toll on my pregnant body.

As with all graduations on large university campuses, the whole procedure was long and boring. When it finally came time for my brother to walk, he looked like every other black gown clad graduate. The only way I knew it was him was by the announcement of his name. I almost missed him, as his first name, George, was used. I caught the name Kurtz just in time to focus on the stage. As he received his hood, my thoughts journeyed back to the years when he was a rebellious high school student. Only our mother had seen his potential. Now, sixteen years after her death, that potential was being fulfilled. I sent a silent message down to the stage. *Mom would be proud.*

After the ceremony, we joined the crowds making their way out of the auditorium. How would we find Robert and Carol in all this pandemonium? People were milling around as families tried to find their graduates. Carol saw us first, calling out and waving. We probably stood out as the only mixed couple in the crowd. Dad was with her, and I gave him a hug. We moved to one side to wait for Robert to join us. My first thought as I caught sight of him was: *he's grown a beard.* The second was *He's losing his hair, and he's only 38.*

I wondered why my thoughts weren't more centered on the significance of the moment rather than what he looked like. Was I afraid of making a mistake and screwing up our reunion? Robert showed immediately that the past eleven years had given him a maturity and confidence that he lacked as a young man. He immediately knelt down to greet our son and introduce himself as his uncle. Jason seemed shy as he looked at this stranger who was kneeling before him. He did say quietly, "Hi." I was definitely getting emotional looking at my brother and son together. Robert would be his only uncle, as Pat was an only child. Uncle Leland had said that family relations would be more important as the years passed. He was right.

Standing, Robert then shook hands with Pat. Everything went seamlessly from that point. Dad, looking on, must have silently rejoiced that his years as a go-between were over. Making our way to the motel where they were staying, Robert and Pat immediately retired to the bar for their own private moment. I could only imagine what that conversation was like. Later, Pat told me that Robert apologized for prejudging our marriage, saying he would understand if Pat did not accept his apology. Their conversation didn't last long. Just time for them to have a drink and decide that the past was best forgotten. In that short time, our futures took a new turn. I finally had all my family back! In the forty years since, much has changed. But my brother remains a part of our lives.

We continued on to Missouri that same day. My father flew back the next day, so he was there to greet us when we arrived. We enjoyed the Bicentennial festivities. Jason got a kick out of the hayride and the horses in the parade. He wasn't that happy with the fried fish, but then most five-years-olds are picky eaters. Pat and I got to spend time with my aunts, uncles and cousins. We loved the fish fry. Dad was working in the Kiwanis tent and personally fried our dinners. The sermon by the Lincoln lookalike was actually pretty good. The entertainment on the bandstand was high quality for a town the size of Oregon. There were some talented people in my hometown. More importantly, the two hundredth celebration of our country was also my celebration of the reconciliation with my brother.

Seventeen years later, a divorced Robert joined us at Bates College in Maine for Jason's graduation. With him was his new fiance, Marie. Marie was black. Before you think there were two mixed marriages in the family, I need to say that Robert and Marie never married. Robert moved to Illinois to take a job as Assistant Superintendent of Schools in Waukegan. Marie chose to stay in Ohio. Robert did remarry in 1999. He and his wife Barbara live in Florida and travel five months out of the year in their large mobile home. In a sense, 1976 closed the circle that began in 1965 when Pat and I first met.

Those eleven years had treated us kindly. Other people might have had problems with our marriage. Their problems didn't create any for us.

CHAPTER THIRTY-FOUR

TALES TO TELL

These are actually vignettes, not stories. Just a series of short paragraphs that spotlight some of the things that have happened through the years. There are negative ones, informative ones and humorous ones. I'll start with the negative and end with the humorous. I'd rather go out with a smile for my readers.

May 11, 1996. A severe windstorm blew the roof off our house. We had wonderful neighbors who pitched in to help us. One was a roofer who immediately put tarps on the roof to help minimize the water damage. Another allowed us to store furniture in their garage as we tried to move some of the family antiques out of the house. Jason and Stacie were home from school for the summer. For three months, the four of us lived in a motel, compliments of our insurance company.

We got pretty tired of eating out three meals a day. The cats went to a friend's house, my piano went to the tuners and all our belongings from the house went into storage. Fortunately, no one was injured. Jason was clerking for a judge at the county seat and needed a car. Pat's work was thirty miles away. My job was in the same town as the motel, so he dropped me off each morning and picked me up each night. Stacie was able to walk to her job in a card/gift shop at a local mall. Jason would pick her up when she worked nights. We moved back into the house in August, just in time to send the kids off to school. What a summer that was!

May 1982. Pat and I had been married for fifteen years and lived in upstate New York. Our children were eleven and five. Pat's mother came for her twice yearly visit from her home in Washington, D.C. I had never had a good relationship with my mother-in-law. We were just too different. She didn't hesitate to criticize the way I cooked and even the way I made the beds. The way I did things was the way I learned from my mother. In my mind, when she criticized me, she was criticizing my mother. That did not sit well. It came to a head one day when Pat was at work and the kids were in school. It was my day off, and Carol was visiting us from D.C. She was sitting on the couch watching her soap operas. I was getting ready to go upstairs when out of the blue she looked me in the eye and said, “You have two rotten children who will never grow up to be worth anything.” It was as if time stood still. I could hear my heart beating. My chest was tight, and I could hardly breathe. The world was getting black, and I grabbed the railing of the staircase to keep from falling. Then anger flashed through me as sharp and bright as lightning. I took a deep breath, stood straight and tall, and said right back at her, “At least we're raising them and not putting them in a foster home like you did”.

She left that night for her sister's in Brooklyn. When we went to Washington to spend Thanksgiving with her, the incident wasn't mentioned. She passed away four months later. I never understood what would make her say something like that. As far as I know, our children had never done anything to upset her. Perhaps she was in the early stages of some form of dementia and didn't fully comprehend what she was saying or realize the consequences.

I'm not sure of the exact date of this next incident. I do know Stacie was in high school and Jason was away at college. I received a phone call from a woman in the Bronx asking questions about prejudice and discrimination in Florida, New York and its school system. How she got my name and phone number or how she knew our children were black I never found out. I was honest and said that in the sixteen years we had lived in Florida, we had never had any incidents of bias or prejudice.

That black family moved to Florida and bought a house just

down the street from us. I can only describe her two sons as young thugs. The oldest threatened to kill Stacie and menaced Stacie and I with a baseball bat. He later murdered a mentally retarded boy and went to prison. They brought their problems with them from the Bronx and infected the stability of our little town with their own hatred and disregard for the lives and rights of others. If the mother hoped moving out of the Bronx would save her sons, she was mistaken.

End of negative and on to informative. Pat's mother and grandmother were both educated at Tuskegee Institute in Tuskegee, Alabama. Their tuition was fully paid by the Stokes family of New York City who were supporters of the school. There was speculation that Pat's grandmother, Pearl, was in some way connected with the Stokes family. Nothing was ever proven.

There are two stories associated with how our daughter Stacie got her name. Pat said he recognized the name of the doctor who delivered me when we were getting our marriage license. He knew Dr. Winton T. Stacy when he was stationed at the Ft. Leavenworth Army Hospital in the early 1960's. I remember that when we went to visit Ft. Leavenworth in 1968, Dr. Stacy's name was on the roster of the hospital's doctors. Pat was looking for names from when he was stationed there. He immediately recognized Dr. Stacy's name. I said, "That's the doctor who delivered me!"

It's hard to believe that Pat worked with the doctor who

delivered me. I never met Dr. Stacy but was so struck by the coincidence that we decided to name our daughter Stacie. The *ie* ending was my idea. Dr. Stacy was the one who got me safely into this world. After my mother's nine miscarriages, she was told not to try again. Her health was in jeopardy. Dr. Stacy put her to bed for the last six months of her pregnancy with me. Thank you, Dr. Stacy!

Jason received the Benjamin E. Mays Scholarship from Bates College in 1989. Dr. Mays was a graduate of Bates, the President of Morehouse College, and a mentor of Dr. Martin Luther King, Jr., who attended Morehouse. The scholarship went to a black student of merit. It was a full four-year scholarship that paid not only for tuition, but also room and board. Stacie received several small scholarships during her undergraduate years at Keene State College. When she graduated with honors in 1999, she was the recipient of the Jenkins Scholarship for graduate school. We have two smart kids.

The Thurber Pound Cake is famous in Pat's family. No one knows exactly where the original recipe came from, but we suspect his grandmother, Pearl. Everyone in his family makes the Thurber Pound Cake for holidays and family get-togethers. It has a secret ingredient that gives it a unique flavor. I have never made it. Pat is always the one who bakes it, and he has passed the recipe on to Stacie. She's made it a few times, but says hers never turns out as good as her father's. She's an excellent cook. Maybe she just needs a little more practice.

Now for the humor. Pat's first cousin, Stephen, told the following. Their cousin Carolyn was married to Boogie who worked for the CIA. At one point in the 1980's, he was the bodyguard for the CIA Director, Bill Casey. Talking to the director when they were in the Reagan White House, Boogie said, "Isn't America great? It's the only nation in the world where a black man with a gun can be in the white House." Don't know if President Obama carried a gun when he was in the White House thirty years later, but there were certainly black Secret Service agents who did. Boogie was one of the two blacks first hired by the CIA.

Back in the early 1980's Robert, Pat and I took turns taking my father to Minnesota fishing. In his eighties, he was no longer able to make the long drive by himself. Robert took the first week to get him to Battle Lake. Pat took the middle week, and I did the final week and brought him home. The first year, Jason went with his father. Pat found himself the motor man for all the trips out on the lake fishing. He had never run an outboard motor in his life. Getting away from the dock and traveling out to a fishing spot was no trouble at all. By the time they were ready to go in, Pat felt he had mastered this new skill. He was soon to discover that he still had much to learn. Bringing the boat into the dock where many other boats were tied up takes some maneuvering. He tried time and again to get their boat close enough to the dock, but kept bumping into the dock and having to start over. Willard and Jason watching those attempts, were doubled over with laughter. He finally succeeded in docking the boat but remembers the experience as one of the embarrassing moments in his life.

In my job as Recreation Therapist at a local health facility, I planned almost two hundred activities a month for the residents. One month, I scheduled a pancake breakfast for the men and put it as an Aunt Jemima breakfast on the monthly calendar. Boy, did that raise a stink. There were complaints to the administrator that I was prejudiced. It was the only time in my almost fifty year marriage to a black man that I had ever been called prejudiced!

There are probably hundreds of other little tales that could be told about our mixed marriage and our families. The time has come, however, to bring our story to a close. In forty-nine years, we have lived, loved and thrived. We never let other people's prejudices interfere with the way we lived our lives. I like to think our love for each other protected us from those who looked at us with bias. We always felt if we didn't respond negatively to any prejudice, it couldn't become our problem. The negativity was all on the other side. Many loving thoughts go out to those who have passed on and all those still with us who supported us and helped us through the years. I wrote the following to Pat in 1967 when he was in the hospital with dangerously high blood pressure. To me, it summarizes our marriage and love for each other. *You have given me the cherished privilege of sharing a portion of your life, Pat, and so I must share both the ups and the downs, the happiness and the uncertainty. To love is to feel with and not just about the other person, and I do love you, Pat, so much that nothing else matters just as long as you are well, happy and content to let me continue sharing that which can only be yours to give. Get well, knowing that we have in each other all happiness and joy.*

EPILOGUE

While Pat and I knew each other almost two years before we got married, we discovered that you don't really get to know a person until you're married. Each of us has depths that it has taken over fifty years to fully explore. Without going into specifics, I'll just say that as we approach our fiftieth anniversary, I have come to the conclusion that our differences are what has made our marriage so successful. Pat sees the big picture. I fill in the details. Between the two of us, we cover the entire surface of our world.

When we celebrated our twenty-fifth wedding anniversary in 1992, we were just one of about 231,000 interracial couples in the United States. Today, we are about one in 1,375,000 of such couples. Those figures come from the latest census. That doesn't mean there is no more prejudice or discrimination. In fact, the racial climate in 2016 as I write this is worse than it has been in decades. Looking at the news or reading the papers, you find daily stories about racial incidents throughout the country. It is our hope that people with clearer minds and caring hearts will help move the country toward more understanding and tolerance.

Pat and I have long been retired and now live in Delaware in a 55 and Older Complex. Pat, at age 80, is still involved with his photography. His weekly trips to the beach with his Nikon give him great shots to photoshop on the computer. At 76, I lead an exercise class at a senior center and do volunteer music programs at area health facilities. Pat has been diagnosed with Multiple Myeloma, a form of blood cancer but so far is beating the odds. He remains active and involved in his family and the world around him. My main problem is arthritis. Probably a result of all that dancing when I was young. Or it could just be old age. The strength of our love has not dimmed as we approach our fiftieth wedding anniversary in 2017.

Our son, Jason, is a lawyer with a nonprofit watch dog firm in Washington, D.C. He deals mostly with "freedom of information" issues. He graduated from William and Mary with his law degree and has been with the same firm for nineteen years. His wife, Karla, is from the Philippines and is a nurse. She became a citizen in 2013. They live in Maryland, so we see them often.

Stacie and our granddaughter, Ariana, live in Orlando, Florida.

Stacie has her Masters and works as an online manager for a large university. Despite the distance, we see them four times a year.

We finally made it back to Europe after almost forty-seven years. Our trips in 2014 and 2015 brought back wonderful memories. Of course, it's now the European Union with the Euro. We actually saw countries like Hungary and the Czech Republic that we missed in the sixties as they were behind the Iron Curtain. The best part, however, was visiting Trier and all the small towns along the Moselle River that were our haunts fifty years ago.

I'll close with the following. In 2014 we won a *Not So Newly Wed Game* on Valentine's Day. We won handily against two other couples. We should have, considering we've known each other all these wonderful years!

Made in the USA
Coppell, TX
23 September 2020

Made in the USA
Coppell, TX
23 September 2020